901 SUPER QUICK SEWING TIPS

.... and THEY SEWED FIG LEAVES
TOGETHER and MADE THEMSELVES
APRONS ....

GENESIS 3:7

TABLE OF CONTENTS

May the ANGELS spread SUNSHINE on your Sewing Machine
and GOLDUST on YOUR THIMBLE

MANY THANKS to my SEWING FRIENDS who took the time to share their TIPS and SUGGESTIONS, helping to make the REVISED EDITION of SUPER QUICK SEWING TIPS a reality.

MARGARET P. BEALS, Marshfield, MA
CAROLYN BLUM, San Jose, CA
FLORENCE CAPRON, Los Gatos, CA
MRS. JOEL COLEMAN, Medford, NJ
MRS. RUSSELL DIXON, Brooklyn, NY
ALFREDA FATUM, Queens Village, NY
MRS. L. G. FISHER, Dumfries, VA
GRACE L. GATES, Somerset, NJ
GERALDINE A. GRAY, Brooklyn, NY
VONDA HIBSHMAN, Pismo Beach, CA
AGNES E. HOFER, Rosemead, CA
HELEN M. KRISTUFEK, Torrance, CA
JUNE LEWIS, Ventura, CA
ELEANOR J. JONES, Phoenix, AZ
MARY LUCK, Dallas, TX
RUTH E. LUKE, Monterey, CA
DOROTHY L. MATOUSEK, Santa Monica, CA
HILDI MEYER, Los Angeles, CA
BARBARA D. MICKELS, Irving, TX
MARY MOORE, Houston, TX
DONNA J. MURPHY, Sultan, WA
MRS. DAVID PECORA, Wilmington, DE
L. FAYE POWELL, Evansville, IN
MARY ROEVER, Hingham, MA
MARGARET E. SCHOEN, South River, NJ
LILLIAN L. SCHAFFER, Grand Island, NY
MRS. RONNIE SPURLOCK, Inola, OK
PATTI STAUFFER, Sarasota, FL
PATRICIA WELLS, North Adams, MI

ILLUSTRATIONS – DIANA L. ANDERSON

COVER – MONA EVANS

EDITING – NELSENE DeRANIAN

Original Edition SUPER QUICK SEWING TIPS

FIRST PRINTING Fall 1980
SECOND PRINTING Spring 1981
THIRD PRINTING Fall 1981
FOURTH PRINTING Spring 1982
FIFTH PRINTING Spring 1983

Revised Edition – 901 SUPER QUICK SEWING TIPS
FIRST PRINTING January 1984

A PLACE OF YOUR OWN

1. ORGANIZE YOUR FABRICS ...

If you're a true FABRI-HOLIC, there's FABRIC in

.. cupboards
.. closets
.. cars
.. the re-
.. frigerator
.. garage
.. and ..
sometimes
there's
fabric in
"his"
chest of
drawers.

There's
fabric
"stashed"
even at
your
best
friend's
house
'cause
you were
afraid
to bring
it home.

"He" says
you have
too much
already;
however, you know you didn't have **THAT** color
when buying the last piece.

Use a rainy day. Lay out all fabric by color. Put coordinating prints with solids.

Cut a small swatch of each. Tape by color to pages in a looseleaf notebook. Below each swatch, write fabric content, width and yardage. Put a care instruction label alongside each swatch.

KEEP the notebook up to date with swatches and informa- tion on subsequent purchases. Remove the swatch when fabric is made up.

To coordinate new purchases with what you have already, take the notebook shopping.

2. SPACE SAVER ... Everyone seems to be further ahead with fabric than time to make it up. We simply run out of space for storage of "future garments."

Cut a strip of heavy paper (grocery bag will do) about 3 1/2" wide and long enough to wrap the fabric roll **TWICE**. **Roll the fabric.**

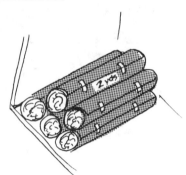

Secure paper around the roll with tape. Write **yardage amount, care instruction, fibre content, etc.** on the paper. **Fabric is easier to stack in rolls.**

3. FABRIC MAY BE STORED IN GARMENT STORAGE BAGS. They're roomy and long enough to hold different yardage lengths.

Use skirt hangers to clip fabrics like velvet, corduroy, etc. Pin information on the fabric, showing **width, yardage, care instruction** and whether pretreated. Everything can be seen by merely unzipping the bag.

4. DO NOT FOLD LEATHER-LIKE fabrics for storage.

Roll and place in an empty cylindrical tube. A **LARGE** Christmas wrapping cardboard tube comes in handy.

5. STORE UNFINISHED PROJECTS IN A SUITCASE ... or see-thru shirt box.

Be sure everything goes in, i.e. pattern, cut out garment, interfacing, etc.

6. ORGANIZE LIKE YOUR SEWING ROOM WAS A WHOLE KINGDOM.

Have an area in the house that is <u>ALL</u> yours. It should be small and everything within reach.

The ironing board should be adjustable. Keep it near the sewing machine so you can turn from machine to board without getting up.

A cotton ironing board cover should be used when pressing knits or synthetics. Some covers hold heat. A garment may be melted in spots, even though the iron had a correct setting.

DO have lots of **LIGHT**. If necessary, put an adjustable lighting device on the sewing table.

7. A FULL LENGTH MIRROR IS AN ABSOLUTE MUST.

8. SEWING TABLE SHOULD BE THE RIGHT HEIGHT FOR YOU.

   Shoulder and backaches are no fun. (My table is an old door laid across two wine barrels cut off to suit my sewing height).

9. SIT COMFORTABLE ... Get a swivel chair, adjustable to your size. If thread builds up around chair rollers, run a saw blade in crevices to remove.

10. Put a clear, plastic type cover on the sewing machine table. Pattern instruction and other written items may be slipped underneath. They're easy to see; don't get lost and area stays neat.

11. If sewing room does not have carpet, you may be competing with the machine foot control for "runner of the year" award.

    To keep it in "it's place" cut a rubber typewriter mat in half. Place one half under the foot control.

12. To avoid SHOULDER and BACKACHE, CUTTING TABLE should be the same height as your HIPBONE.

13. Put CORKBOARD on the wall in back of your sewing machine for instant "pinups," pattern pieces, belt loops and other little "losables."

14. Fold a LARGE BATH TOWEL and place underneath the sewing machine. It serves the dual purpose of grounding the machine AND is a handy PINCUSHION.

3

15. Also, machine won't dance around if piece of CARPET or RUBBER TYPEWRITER cushion is placed underneath ... <u>OR</u> ...

Make your own PAD from pretty quilted fabric. Put JIFFY GRIP or JAR RINGS on the bottom.

16. One of my sewing friends had an 8' x 4' quarter inch pegboard cut in half. One part (2' x 4') was fitted with all types hooks for hanging instruction guide, thread spools, needles, scissors and other notions. Everything can be seen and reached in an instant.

The other part was used as a cutting board.

It was placed on top of the ironing board. Height could be adjusted.

17. Make a FUNCTIONAL sewing/cutting table that's out of the way when not in use.

Attach <u>PLYWOOD</u> to the wall with hinges. The table should have detachable legs. Cover top side (in <u>DOWN</u> position) with muslin, white felt or similar fabric. Fabric will not slip when cutting/sewing.

On the reverse side, put a painting or other artwork with frame. It's pretty when table is in the **up** position.

18. Gather and place together <u>all</u> items needed for the sewing project.

Looking for notions after the project starts is a "time" and "enthusiasm" killer.

19. <u>GO TO A GARAGE SALE or CLEAN OUT YOUR OWN ...</u>

Use what you have already, for sewing gear. Saves money.

... Get an old see-through SHOEBAG to hold NOTIONS, SCISSORS, etc.

... Give a little boy $1.00 to round up an old discarded tool box. Paint it a cheerful color and put sewing gear in all the cubicles.

... Use a CIGAR BOX for small items.

... See-through SHIRT or SHOE BOXES in the back of "his" closet have lots of uses.

... Store PATTERNS or FABRICS in an UNUSED TOY BOX, long outgrown by the young man who is now too big to be kissed in public by "mama."

... Use PLASTIC BOXES; they're found in lots of places.

... Cover an old NIGHTSTAND with FABRIC SCRAPS and put HOOKS all over. Let it stand in the sewing room with notions hanging from every angle, within easy reach of the sewing machine.

... Claim the neighbor's discarded SERVING CART. Roll it from room to room with all your sewing projects.

... PLASTIC VEGETABLE BINS COME in handy for stacking fabric.

... Put a COAT or CUP RACK on the sewing wall. Small things can be hung.

... Substitute an old MAKEUP TRAY to hold PINS, NEEDLES, TWEEZERS and "LITTLE LOSABLES."

... Visualize any DISCARD that may be useful in your sewing room.

... Keep a COASTER on the sewing table for an extra cup of COFFEE. It tastes so good and calms your nerves after sewing the sleeve in, WRONG side out.

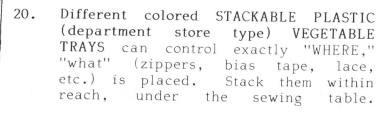

20. Different colored STACKABLE PLASTIC (department store type) VEGETABLE TRAYS can control exactly "WHERE," "what" (zippers, bias tape, lace, etc.) is placed. Stack them within reach, under the sewing table.

21. Tape ends of RIBBON, RICKRACK, TAPE and other long sewing pieces to an empty paper towel or toilet

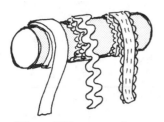

tissue roll. Wrap around the roll and pin or tape the other end. Several colors can be put on one roll.

22. Fill empty TISSUE BOXES with cotton, fiberfill or other stuffing used in sewing projects. It comes in handy on the sewing table.

23. Buying a NEW SEWING MACHINE? Get one that has a removable plate. Use of a **FREE ARM** shortens sewing time when putting in sleeves, sewing in small areas and circles.

24. If there is not enough time to finish a sewing project, put everything in a large **PLASTIC BOWL or BOX**. Leave it on the sewing table. It will "nudge" every time you walk by.

FABRIC KNOWLEDGE

25. Until experienced, sew ONLY on fabrics you like. It takes a long time to make any garment from "UNLOVED" fabric.

26. Watch your FABRIC BUYING HABITS ...

   ... Does the COLOR do anything for you?
   ... Do you LOVE it and can you look at it every day for six weeks without getting tired of it?
   ... Will YOU wear the finished garment for a LONG time?
   ... Can you wear the garment with other things in your closet?
   ... Does the PRICE fit your pocketbook?
   ... Do your ACCESSORIES match the fabric?
   ... Will it wrinkle easily?
   ... Will it show soil with only one day's wear?
   ... Will YOU get HIVES and tear your hair when cutting, fitting or sewing it?

27. Buy all FABRIC for one OUTFIT at the same time. There are two reasons for this.

The fabric may be gone by the time you return to buy more.

Bolt dye lots change. Your skirt may be one color and the jacket another, if fabric is not purchased from the SAME bolt.

6

28. Do not test the STRETCH of KNITS on bias or diagonal.

 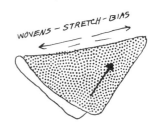

With wovens, diagonal or bias stretch is the greatest. With knits, diagonal or bias has the least amount of stretch.

29. HOW TO DETERMINE FABRIC STRETCH ... Fold the fabric HORIZONTALLY. Place tapemeasure alongside the fold.

STRETCH 10" of fabric to:	FABRIC STRETCH is:
12 1/2"	25%
15"	50%
17 1/2"	75%
20"	100%

Always compare with specifications on the pattern envelope and make purchases accordingly.

30. ACETATE fabric will dissolve in fingernail polish. If there's any question about the fabric content, apply small drop of polish on a scrap. If it melts, it's acetate.

31. INTERLOCKING STITCHES ... There is a lot of INTERLOCKING STITCH fabric on the market. THERE IS NOTHING WRONG WITH THEM. They're beautiful and you should know how to work with this type fabric.

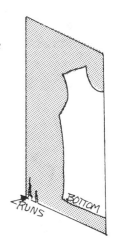

Under "pressure" interlocking stitch fabrics will RUN (or zipper) from the BOTTOM. They do NOT "run" from the TOP.

To find the BOTTOM, slightly stretch lower raw edge at the selvage. If it "runs" that's the bottom. If it doesn't "run," try the other end.

To avoid problems with interlocking stitch fabrics, cut it right. PLACE BOTTOM PIECE OF THE PATTERN at BOTTOM of the FABRIC.

Generally, there is no pressure on garment hemlines after completion; so "worry" about "runners" is eliminated. Use of a FUSIBLE WEB for HEMMING insures "no run." DO TEST A SCRAP before using fusible web on the hem.

32. FABRIC RIGHT and WRONG SIDES ...

   KNITS ... Tiny holes are alongside the edges. Holes are pushed in from the RIGHT side.

   WOVENS ... RIGHT side has more finished looking selvage

   If you still can't tell, keep a magnifying glass handy. Through the glass, RIGHT side looks more finished.

33. Most WOVEN NYLON fabrics will fray badly. SEAR edges with a candle before sewing.

34. Stretch WOVEN fabric is NOT the same as KNIT. Regular patterns designed for WOVENS should be used.

35. SILK is "ALLERGIC" to chloride salts contained in some foods, perspiration and salt water, which weaken the fibres. Use this knowledge accordingly.

36. SILK will turn YELLOW if left to dry in the air.

37. Be careful when using STEAM on SILK. Water spots may appear.

38. Dyes used in SILK are sensitive to both natural and artificial light. If continuously exposed to light, silk will droop and become misshapen. Silk should not be used for window coverings, EVER.

*39. Sewing with SILK and very fine fabrics is a new and different world. It is suggested you do special reading if you sew with silk/fine fabrics regularly.

40. Next time a cold weather garment is needed, try THINSULATE

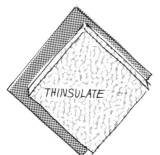

It won't mat, bunch or thin out with use. It retains warmth even when wet. It CAN REPLACE DOWN in ski and outerwear. (Use it as polyester fiberfill yardage. SCRIM side should be placed away from the outer fabric shell).

KNOWING ABOUT PATTERNS

41. LIST NUMBERS and DESCRIBE all PATTERNS in a looseleaf notebook. Lessens the risk of spending $ for two just alike.

*(Suggested reading: SEWING WITH SILK and OTHER FINE FABRICS by Jane Shaner).

42. Never throw away OLD PATTERNS. Some patterns become collectors' items. Also, use them to experiment. Sometimes, pattern pieces are interchangeable. That EXPENSIVE dress in ready-to-wear may be made with interchanged pattern pieces.

43. Put an INFORMATION SHEET in the pattern envelope. Attach fabric swatch of the garment. List alterations. Swatch identifies the garment and you will know what needs to be done next time pattern is used.

44. Iron an INTERFACING STRIP to a SCRAP from each garment. Write NAME and NUMBER of the pattern used to make the garment, on interfaced side.

    If you're not happy with the garment, you know what adjustments to make in the future. If garment fits, you're comfortable in using the pattern again.

45. Don't just count on your LUCK. Some patterns are designed for knits only. Some are designed for wovens only. Use KNIT PATTERNS for KNITS and WOVEN PATTERNS for WOVENS.

46. It's a "NO-NO" to pin a pattern together for fit, before cutting the fabric. Tissue paper never fits peaks and valleys, lumps and bumps or "corners" of the human anatomy. If you have doubts about the pattern fit, cut major pieces from muslin, worn out sheet or remnants and test-fit.

    Sometimes, remnants can be purchased for a minimum. It doesn't matter if each pattern piece is cut from a different color remnant.

47. Cut out styles you like from catalogs and old pattern books. Paste in YOUR IDEA BOOK. Write the number of a similar pattern you have already, under the style in YOUR book. Sometimes, you can get ideas on how to create a new look to one of your old patterns.

48. Have a PATTERN PARTY. Invite friends to bring patterns no longer needed or wanted. Exchange or sell the patterns for a nominal sum. It's a lot of fun.

49. It's next to impossible to put a USED PATTERN in the same envelop in which it was purchased.

Cut and paste the envelope **FRONT** to the front of a large 10" x 12" mailing envelope. Repeat with the back. Pattern folds easier in larger folds and goes into the mailing envelope that is more durable. It will last twice as long as the pattern envelope.

50. <u>STORAGE FOR PATTERNS</u> ... Roll the pattern. Place in an empty cardboard PAPER TOWEL or CHRISTMAS PAPER tube. Label contents on outside. Put in a safe place so it isn't thrown away as trash ...OR... use MILK CARTONS to store patterns. It depends upon the pattern envelope size. Avoid crushing the pattern.

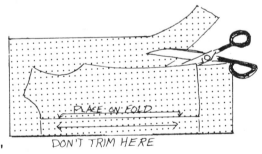

51. Use a HI-LITER(r) pen to mark your size, corresponding yardage requirements and notions on back of the pattern envelope. Without wading through all sizes, requirements are seen instantly.

52. Keep a roll of <u>WAX PAPER</u> near the sewing table and ironing board. It can be substituted for pattern paper by ironing several sheets together.

53. Tissue patterns can be made PERMANENT with <u>PERMA PATTERN</u>. It's fused to the tissue. Easy to mark since it's transparent.

54. PRIOR TO CUTTING OUT, ALWAYS <u>PRESS</u> out wrinkles in tissue paper patterns with a <u>dry iron</u>. <u>NO STEAM</u>. Steam may cause the paper to shrink or develop holes.

55. Trim EXCESS TISSUE on patterns before laying pieces on fabric.

EXCEPTION: Leave excess tissue in place along "FOLD" line as an additional re- minder that pattern piece is to be placed on the "fold."

56. <u>PATTERN MAKING, ALTERING and CUTTING OUT should be done in a QUIET area.</u> It's very difficult to watch soap operas and alter at the same time.

Do <u>BE HAPPY</u> when sewing. Negative emotions distort judgment and affects creativity.

Tune in to your most FAVORITE and LIVELY music. It improves disposition and makes "happy hands."

10

57. If the pattern has a separate front facing or pieces that can be joined with a STRAIGHT SEAM, speed up the process. Position and pin pattern pieces together on SEAMLINES. Cut as one piece from the fabric.

58. Make and have a STANDARD WAIST BAND on hand for YOU. Saves time in alter- ing each new pattern.

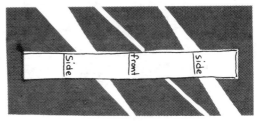

Cut GROSGRAIN RIBBON to fit your waist. Mark sides and center front with indel- ible ink. Place on waistband pattern piece when cutting and transfer construction marks.

59. Timesaver for LAYING and CUTTING out PATTERNS ... If making more than one garment and fabric purchased is less than all pattern requirements, BETTER lay out all pieces before cutting.

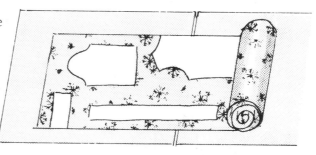

If there's no time to cut after layout, place two cutting boards on the floor end to end. Spread fabric and lay out all pattern pieces. Then roll all pattern pieces inside the fabric and put away until cutting time.

When it's time to cut, merely unroll. Pieces are in order. "Picking up" and "putting down" time is saved and you didn't lose the pattern pieces.

60. PRECUT all pattern pieces accurately, as opposed to just separating them. This allows for fitting pieces more closely on fabric and saves yardage. It also aids in more accurate pattern alteration.

61. When TRIMMING PATTERNS, allow a small margin along any "FOLD" line. The tiny margin is a double reminder that fabric is to be cut on the "fold."

62. Save a little PATTERN MONEY. Extend the basic blouse to dress length.

63. Use MULTI-SIZE PATTERNS for children's clothes. Saves money when larger size is needed as the child grows.

64. If pattern has LONG and SHORT hemline, don't cut off the long part to get the short pattern.

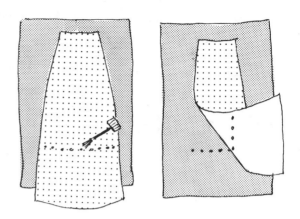

Puncture the short hem cutting line with a machine needle. Mark punctured areas with a marking pen, liquid paper or chalk.

Cut fabric on markings. Leave long pattern intact.

65. Another way to keep the long length of a multi-length pattern intact.

From each side, cut in one third the distance on cutting line of the short version.   Leave center one third UNCUT.

66. Make your FAVORITE HANDBAG PATTERN easy to use. Convert it to CARDBOARD. Just lay cardboard pattern on the fabric. Trace around it and cut. QUICK and EASY.

67. Rip an old favorite garment apart. Press pieces and use as a pattern. Make notations on the pieces with a marking pen.

Watch the seam allowances if garment was purchased. Ready-to-wear often shorts the seam allowances.

NOTIONS KNOWLEDGE

68. Before winding THREAD onto the bobbin, run first 8" across a different color CRAYON, four or five times. Crayon color will alert you when the bobbin thread is about to run out.

69. Fill a DOZEN BOBBINS (all at the same time) with MOST FREQUENTLY used THREADS. They're handy when needed.

70. Put MATCHING BOBBIN and SPOOL THREADS TOGETHER. Handi-Bob Plastic Clips attach to the spool top and will hold BOBBIN in place. (Ask Viking Sewing Machine Dealers about Handi-Bobs).

If spindles on THREAD PEG BOARD are long enough, put bobbins on top of the spools, matching thread colors.

71. Presser Foot should be in <u>RAISED POSITION</u> when BOBBIN is being filled or thread may break. If BOBBIN is filled beyond "FULL" point, upper thread will break when sewing begins.

72. <u>ALWAYS FILL AN EMPTY BOBBIN.</u> If you start with a partially filled bobbin, thread will wind unevenly. Stitches will be uneven.

73. Using <u>BENT BOBBINS</u> will cause uneven stitches.

Check to see if BOBBIN is bent by rolling it across the table. If bobbin wobbles, don't use it.

74. After finishing the garment, use "LEFTOVER" BOBBIN THREAD to make tailor tacks.

75. Claim a discarded hollow, rubber ball. Cut a 2" slit in the side.

It stores little items like hooks & eyes, snaps, buttons and thimbles. To open, press each end of the slit, simultaneously.

76. Put loose HOOKS, EYES, SNAPS and small items on a strip of transparent tape. Stick to the notions board. Easily seen and very handy.

77. Put unmatched or loose SNAPS, PANT HOOKS and other LOSABLES in a BABY FOOD JAR.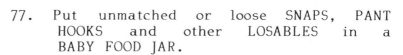

78. Put CHEESECLOTH between SNAP SECTIONS. Hang on the sewing board.

79. Cut a slit in the plastic pocket on "LITTLE LOSABLE"

packages (such as Pant Hooks). After use, if there are remaining LOSABLES, put transparent tape over the slit.

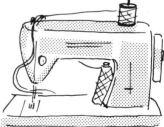

PANT OR SKIRT HOOK

80.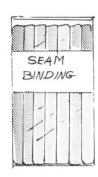

SEAM BINDING

Keep SEAM BINDING, HEM TAPE and similar packaged items in - tact and neat.

Make a horizontal slit in one end of the package. Carefully remove from the package. Use needed amount and return un-used portion. If necessary, place small piece of transparent tape over the slit end.

81. Keep a supply of each SIZE NEEDLE on hand. Nothing is more frustrating or time consuming than a broken needle and "stores are closed."

82. When CHANGING MACHINE NEEDLE, place a small MIRROR on the face plate. It's easier to see what you're doing.

83. DO NOT USE DULL NEEDLES or PINS. Put a NEW NEEDLE in the machine with each new garment project.

84. BALLPOINT NEEDLES and PINS should be used when sewing with KNITS.

85. Know which NEEDLE is which. Put a dot of bright fingernail polish on ALL BALLPOINT NEEDLES.

86. Rubbing CHALK over the printed "SIZE" of a sewing machine needle makes it easier to see.

87. For TOPSTITCHING, use a NEEDLE one size larger than was used to sew the garment.

88. TOPSTITCHING NEEDLES specifically designed for HEAVY topstitching are now available. Ask at your fabric shop.

89. Write the SIZE NEEDLE in the sewing machine on a small piece of masking tape. Place it on the machine. No more guessing what needle was left in the machine.

90. If a DOUBLE NEEDLE is necessary for the project but the machine does not have the extra spool stick/spindle, use THREAD on a LARGE CONE. Cone should be heavy enough to set on the table in back of the machine. Doesn't work with small cones.

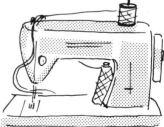

91. HARD TO THREAD THE MACHINE NEEDLE? ...

... Place **PRESSER FOOT** in the **DOWN** position. Presser Foot shank will cast a reflection through the needle's eye and it's easier to see ...

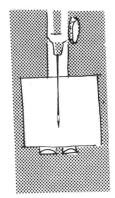

... Hold a **WHITE** slip of paper in back of the needle. (Be sure the needle has been properly inserted in the machine).

... Cut the **THREAD** on a **SLANT** ...

... Slip both ends of the thin strip of plastic from a gum/cigarette package through needle's eye. Place thread in the strip loop and pull ends toward the back ...

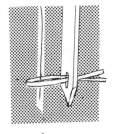

... Remove needle from the machine. Thread and replace ...

... Cut **THREAD** near the spool spindle. Replace thread with a new spool. Tie new color to old machine thread. Pull old thread at needle's eye.

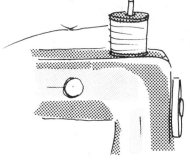

New thread follows because it has been tied to the old.

Knot should be **SMALL** as possible. Works well with Size 11 or larger needles. Even if knot does not go through needle's eye, rest of the threading process is speedy.

92. USE THE RIGHT NEEDLE ...

Sharp pointed needles should be used on **WOVENS**. Ballpoint needles should be used on **KNITS** (rounded point does not pierce knit fabric). Wedge shaped needles should be used to sew **LEATHERS and VINYLS**.

BE GUIDED by the THREAD & NEEDLE CHART
provided on the next page
Courtesy of COATS & CLARK, INC.

93. MATCH and BUY THREAD with FABRIC PURCHASE ...

Thread sews in lighter. Get a shade darker than the fabric color. Holding thread next to the fabric does not mean color will be the same when sewn in.

Thread & Needle Chart

Fabric	J. & P. Coats Thread		J. & P. Coats Needle	
	General Purpose Sewing	Topstitching	Machine Sewing Universal Point	Hand Sewing
Very Lightweight batiste, chiffon, nylon tricot, organza, voile, as well as other sheer fabrics	Dual Duty Plus® Extra Fine	Dual Duty Plus® Extra Fine	size 65 (9)	size 9, 10
Lightweight challis, chambray, crepe, crepe de chine, cotton knits, eyelet, gauze, georgette, gingham, interlock, jersey, percale, seersucker, silk, taffeta		Dual Duty Plus® All-purpose*	size 75 (11)[+]	size 8, 9
Medium-weight broadcloth, brocade, chino, chintz, corduroy, double knit, flannel, linen, oxford cloth, pique, poplin, satin, shantung, suiting, sweatshirt, swimwear, synthetic suedes, terry, velour, velvet, velveteen	Dual Duty Plus® All-purpose*		size 75 (11)[+] or size 90 (14)[+]	size 7, 8
Medium to Heavy-weight coating, denim, double knit, drapery fabric, fake fur, felt, fleece, gabardine, leather, leather-like, quilted fabric, sweater knits, ticking, twill, upholstery fabric		Dual Duty Plus® Topstitching & Buttonhole Twist**	size 90 (14)[+] or size 100 (16)	size 6
Heavy-weight canvas, duck, sailcloth	Dual Duty Plus® Topstitching & Buttonhole Twist**		size 110 (18)	sizes 1-5

Thread & Needle Chart

Special Projects

Hand Quilting	Dual Duty Plus® Hand Quilting or Super Sheen® Cotton Quilting	Betweens/Quilting Hand Needle size 7, 8, 9, or 10
Machine Quilting	Dual Duty Plus® All-purpose*	Universal Point Machine Needle size 90 (14)
Hand Applique	Dual Duty Plus® All-purpose*	Betweens/Quilting Hand Needle size 8 or 9
Machine Applique	Dual Duty Plus® All-purpose* or Dual Duty Plus® Extra Fine	Universal Point Machine Needle size 75 (11)
Hand Sewing on Buttons, Heavy-weight Fabrics, Rug Binding	Dual Duty Plus® Button & Carpet	Embroidery Crewel Hand Needle size 6 or 7
Machine Embroidery	Dual Duty Plus® Extra Fine	Universal Point Machine Needle size 75 (11)

*In addition to Dual Duty Plus® All-purpose cotton-covered polyester core thread, Finesse All-purpose long staple polyester thread or Super Sheen® All-purpose cotton thread may be used.

**Finesse Topstitching Thread may also be used.

†J. & P. Coats Skip-Free Universal Point Needle may also be used when sewing on fabrics where skipped stitches occur.

CHARTS COURTESY OF COATS & CLARK, INC.

Unwind about 4" and press thread into the fabric. Only then should you decide upon the "match."

Some shops do not want you to help yourself to the thread. If assistance is needed, ask.

Molnlycke thread has a slit on top of the spool. With this brand thread, a fingernail may be pushed under the slit and thread will lift out. It does not break, bruise or hurt your finger- nail. It won't even disturb the polish. Method does not work on wooden spools.

**BE KIND TO THE SHOP OWNER. REPLACE THREAD TO THE SPOOL SLIT IF YOU DO NOT BUY.

94. COOKIE JAR in the SEWING ROOM? ... Get a see-through glass cookie jar with metal lid ... the old fashioned kind that has an opening on the front (instead of the top).

Fill it with **thread** and set within reach of your sewing table. It's pretty and front opening really makes "reaching in" easy.

95.

If you've kept the old FOAM WIG HEAD FORM, place large toothpicks or sucker sticks 1 1/4" apart, all over the head. It will be a real conversation piece when the head is covered with spools of colorful thread and bobbins.

96. DELUXE THREAD HOLDER ...

Sew **elastic loops** to sturdy fabric. Tack fabric to a sheet of insulation board. Arrange thread by **color**. Each shade is easy to see.

97. Attach a giant SPICE RACK to the wall in your sewing room just for THREAD. The little shelves are perfect for thread. If your "guy" is handy with tools, have him place dowels on the shelves, long enough to hold spool and bobbin.

98. My grandmother said if THREAD IS FROZEN (yes, in the freezer), it will stay pliable, won't knot or split. She also said it wouldn't KNOT if ironed before use.

99. If you're truly a FABRI-HOLIC, you probably use a lot of the basic thread colors. Save a little $ and time; buy large CONE quantities ... 3,000 - 5,000 yards. You won't run out when the store's closed.

100. SAVE BOXES ,,, Cigar, Wooden Gift Pack, etc. Glue large end of GOLF TEES to inside of the box bottom. Leave enough space between, so thread can be set on the TEES. Make the box pretty by covering with contact paper.

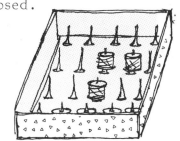

101.  Divide thread into color "families." Store each family in a large ziplock plastic bag. Put all bags in a large, clear glass bowl. Makes a gorgeous decoration for the sewing room. Thread is easy to find.

102. For a neat THREAD DRAWER, sort all thread by basic colors, i.e. blues, yellows, lavenders, etc. Put each color group in a ziplock bag or bag with tie twist.

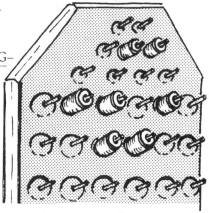

103. THREAD and MATCHED BOBBIN will stay neat if placed in an empty, see-through prescription bottle.

104. PUT THREAD ON A PEGBOARD. Color selection is quick.

105. IF PEGBOARD IS NOT AVAILABLE, use a TRANSPARENT BOBBIN BOX.

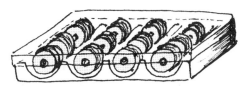 Store it near the thread.

BOBBIN is easy to see for matching spool thread.

106. If it's hard to MATCH bobbin to the thread used last week, keep TWIST TIES handy. When thread is changed, run twist tie through thread and bobbin. They will stay together until needed.

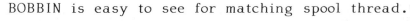

19

107. After use, ALWAYS return loose thread ENDS to the SPOOL SLIT.

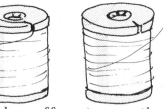

... Saves time
... Avoids waist
... Avoids tangles
... Keeps the sewing box neat.

Should "slit catch" break off, tape thread end to the spool top.

108. DO NOT PUSH HAND NEEDLES THROUGH THREAD ON THE SPOOL.

Thread fibres are cut and will break in several places when used.

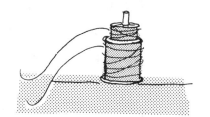

109. MARK THREAD SPOOL SLOT WITH A DARK PERMANENT INK.

110. Substitute two strans of ordinary thread for BUTTONHOLE TWIST. Put spool and bobbin on machine spool spindle. Thread needle with two strands instead of one. (Probably should use a larger needle).

111.

If INVISIBLE THREAD is needed and not available, try using a long strand of hair ... it really works.

112. Wind UNUSED THREAD onto a plastic drinking straw.

Cut off desired length. Place one end into the matching thread spool hole for storage.

To keep thread from ravelling, place end through slit cut in the straw.

113. THREAD WILL STRETCH IF WOUND ON THE BOBBIN TOO FAST. Better to fill the bobbin SLOWLY.

114. COMBINING THREAD COLORS ... Sew MULTICOLOR fabrics, using one color on the spool and another on the bobbin. Colors blend into the fabric better than if only one color is used.

115. CUT THREAD CLOSE TO THE CASE BEFORE REMOVING BOBBIN.

Tension will loosen if thread is continually pulled backward through the case tension spring.

116. Wind <u>REUSABLE THREAD</u> onto PLASTIC LID PIECE from a margarine container. Make a short slit in the "lid" strip to secure thread ends.

117. <u>DO NOT BREAK THREAD. CUT AT AN ANGLE.</u> If there's difficulty in seeing to thread the needle, put a dot of BRIGHT NAIL POLISH on the end.

118. It's frustrating to have thread slipping under the spool, winding around the machine spool spindle. <u>MAKE A THREAD HOLDER.</u> Punch a hole in the center of a shaving cream or deodorant container top. Slip the top onto spool spindle; place thread on the spool spindle. Thread feeds over the top.

119. There's another way to keep thread from slipping under the spool and winding around the spindle.

<u>TAPE A PAPER</u> or <u>STYROFOAM CUP</u> to the back of the sewing machine. Put spool inside the cup.

Also, a PLASTIC DRINKING STRAW may be placed on the spindle. Place an <u>EMPTY</u> spool on the straw spindle. Put thread on top of the <u>EMPTY SPOOL</u>. Really works.

120. To keep THREAD from catching in the SPOOL SLIT when sewing, place "slit" end <u>UP</u> on a vertical spindle. Place "slit" end <u>TOWARD</u> hand wheel on a horizontal spindle.

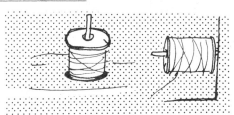

121. If <u>THREAD</u> is "dancing" all over the spindle, put a <u>FELT CIRCLE</u> under the spool ...OR ... put a <u>METAL WASHER</u> on top ... OR ... cut a <u>PLASTIC DRINKING STRAW</u> in half. Put straw over the <u>SPOOL SPINDLE</u>. Place spool on the straw.

122. Save 5 to 15 minutes cutting out time. Use PATTERN WEIGHTS. Pinning can destroy the pattern line and cause fitting problems. If weights are not available,

  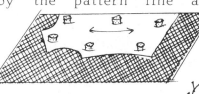

substitute SMALL ROCKS, CANS, PAPERBACK BOOKS, KITCHEN KNIVES or whatever.

Try a little TRANSPARENT TAPE.

123. PUT A PIN- CUSHION on YOUR WRIST ...

It should be comfortable. Takes less time to remove a pin and put it on the wrist. Try it; you'll see.

124. A LARGE PINCUSHION should be kept next to the sewing machine to handle excess pins.

125. Large CANDLE can substitute for a pin- cushion ...

Grandmother said wax helps pins go through the fabric much easier. Keep matches handy in case the lights go out.

126. CIGARETTE FILTER TIP may be used as a temporary CUSHION. Pin it to the corkboard or stuff in center hole of the thread spool.

127. LARGE CORKS may be substitute PINCUSHIONS.

128. Fill the PINCUSHION with used dry coffee grounds. Grounds work as an abrasive. Helps sharpen needles and pins.

129. Make PINCUSHIONS with PLAY SAND. Helps pins and needles stay sharp and it's heavy enough to hold the cushion in place on the sewing table.

130. DO NOT STUFF PINCUSHIONS with polyester fiberfill. It dulls pins and needles.

PINCUSHIONS may be stuffed with SAWDUST or FINE CEDAR SHAVINGS (smells good).

131. Attach a MAGNETIC STRIP to the bottom of a small pincushion. It will stay "put" on the sewing machine.

132. For a TEMPORARY PINCUSHION fold TOWEL SCRAP 3 or 4 times and tape to the machine.

133. Piece of SPONGE makes a handy PINCUSHION ...

Attach to the machine with double sided tape.

134. Cover a ball of STEEL WOOL with pretty fabric and tie with fancy ribbon.

Steel Wool helps keep pins and needles sharp.

135. Sew a piece of JIFFY GRIP or ULTRA SUEDE (Reg. Trade Mark) on the bottom of lightweight, self made PINCUSHIONS to keep them from slipping around on the sewing table.

136. Own TWO pair of GOOD SCISSORS ... They should be sharp enough to cut through FOUR layers of fabric, TO THE POINT. Use NAIL POLISH to mark ONE PAIR with INCHES and FRACTIONS on the outside blade. Saves "picking-up   and putting-down " time when you need to measure.

137. OWN ONE PAIR OF NIPPERS ... Two seconds is saved every time a thread is clipped. It takes longer to pick up scissors, clip and lay them down.

Also, using nippers lessens the chance of inadvertently cutting the garment with sharp scissors.

138. Tie a long cord through one handle or finger rest of NIPPERS and/or SCISSORS.

Attach opposite end to a hook under the sewing table. You won't have to "hunt."

139. Also, SMALL SCISSORS or NIPPERS may be put on a long narrow RIBBON and tied around your neck. Really handy and easily removed.

140. SCISSORS, NIPPERS and other cutting blades will last longer if kept clean and dry. Wipe blades with clean, dry cotton interlock or soft towel after each project.

141. After use, place SCISSORS POINTS in a LARGE CORK.

142. Ever try ELECTRIC SCISSORS? Once the user is accustomed to them, cutting time may be cut about twenty percent.

143. A RUBBER BAND wrapped around handle parts will keep SCISSORS from sliding around on the sewing table.

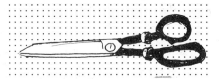

144. Use OLD, EXPENDABLE SCISSORS to CUT METALLIC THREAD. Cutting metal dulls scissors.

145. Scissors will LAST LONGER if a little MACHINE OIL is put on the SCREW occasionally.

146. Put a drop of NEEDLE LUBE on SCISSORS, NIPPERS and other CUTTING BLADES. They will work better.

147. If SCISSORS get BROWN, RUSTY SPOTS, rub HOUSEHOLD AMMONIA... or ... soak brown spots in WHITE VINEGAR. Rub with clean terry cloth.

148. Don't be without an OLFA ROTARY CUTTER. It works better than scissors for some purposes. It has a DISC blade. It cuts curves and circles through several layers of fabric.

149. PINKING SHEARS are great for cutting WOVENS. Straight edge scissors, SHARP TO THE POINT, should be used to cut KNITS.

150. Pinking Shears will cut better (especially on slippery or fine fabrics) if a little PARAFIN or NEEDLE LUBE is applied to the teeth.

Parafin can be brushed off and will not stain. Needle Lube is liquid but, also, will not stain.

151. Choose the ZIPPER with FABRIC PURCHASE. It is very unlikely you will get a perfect color match. USE A DARKER SHADE. At most, it will appear as a shadow.

152. Use ZIPPERS that DO NOT need PRESHRINKING. Steaming should be sufficient.

153. ALWAYS PRESS ZIPPERS before using.

154. Do all ZIPPER FOOT SEWING at one time. Saves the time to change "feet."

155. Use a ZIPPER FOOT to STITCH-IN-THE-DITCH.

156. Use TAPE to put in ZIPPERS. Saves hand tacking time. Apply zipper tape to garment facings. Be sure facing sides are even. Sew in zipper.

157. If the ZIPPER won't "ZIP," rub PARAFIN or soap up and down each side of the teeth.

Scovill markets a little pencil called "EZY GLIDE" that does the same thing.

(Same process will unstick "sticky" windows, drawers, etc.).

158. DOCTOR the SICK ZIPPER ...

Separate bottom of the zipper. Remove metal zipper stop.

Slip "PULL" back onto each side of the zipper. Zip it up.

Sew across zipper bottom where it was separated.

159. Make a SEWING APRON ... Sew a tape-measure along side the hemline. Measuring tool is in your lap.

Put several pockets on the apron to carry small items needed when sewing.

160. Keep EXTRA sewing machine LIGHT BULBS on hand.

161. An EVEN FEED MACHINE FOOT will keep velvets, corduroys and similar fabrics from "creeping" out of control.

162. Singer has a machine foot that moves UPPER fabric piece evenly along as the LOWER piece moves. Works great on slippery and other hard to sew fabrics. Ask at your favorite fabric shop.

163. The WALKING FOOT works very well when sewing slippery or heavy fabrics such as velvet, ultra suede, quilting, etc. It also works well when sewing knit interfacing to small pieces, like collars and cuffs.

164. If machine WALKING FOOT gets TIRED and doesn't walk so well, spray it with WD-40.

165. If PRESSER FOOT gets caught in LOOPY KNIT or HOLE-LY FABRICS, cover and tape "TOES" with small pieces of PLASTIC BAG or CELLOPHANE TAPE.

166. Use FRAY STOP or FRAY CHECK to lock in threads of frayed edges on collars, cuffs, etc.

167. Try the GRABBIT. It's a magnetized heavy PIN TRAY. Pile it high with pins; turn it upside down and shake. Not a single pin is lost. Run it over the carpet to pick up stray pins. They're expensive but really worth having.

168. PUT AN EMERGENCY SEWING KIT IN EACH BEDROOM and BATH ...

   If you don't travel, ask a friend to collect the little complimentary sewing kits available at hotels in larger cities. They have needle, several thread colors, small emery board and buttons.

169. EASY and NICE FASTENER ... Sew fastener to a narrow piece of the garment fabric. Attach to one side of the garment opening. Sew mate to other side of the garment, UNDERNEATH. Easier to snap and unsnap.

170. Get TWICE the mileage from FUSIBLE WEB. Roll a 1" wide strip around two fingers. Slip it off. Cut LENGTH of the strip in half. You will have two 1/2" strips. Narrow and smaller strips work better on lightweight, soft and sheer fabrics.

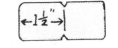

171. When not in use PUT GLUE STICK in the REFRIGERATOR. It will last longer and refrigeration keeps it from getting gummy.

172. As a substitute HEM GAGE, mark off 1 1/2" on a small piece of cardboard. Put a notch in each side.

173. QUILTERS save lots of time with WATER ERASABLE MARKING PENS. Easy to see, if there are sight problems.

174. When not in use, WATER SOLUABLE FABRIC MARKERS should be CAPPED and stored with TIP DOWN. They last longer.

175. There's a PLAID MATCHER on the market. It won't

work on all machines; so check it out before you buy.

It helps eliminate uneven feeding of heavier and slick fabrics like leather, vinyl and velvet. It also helps UPPER and LOWER fabric layers feed more evenly under the presser foot.

176. Make a pretty and <u>INEXPENSIVE WASTEBASKET</u> ... Glue FABRIC SCRAPS on an old bucket, empty ice cream carton or other container ordinarily discarded.

177. For a pretty, economical SEWING BOX, cover a cardboard box with shelf contact paper.

178. Use a MAGNET to pick up stray pins in shag carpet.

179. <u>NEEDLE LUBE</u> can be used on hand needles too. Helps pull the needle through "tough" spots.

180. <u>NEEDLE THREADER</u> will "live" longer ... Put a "smidge" of SUPER GLUE where wires are attached to the holder.

181. Keep a GOOD, SEE-THROUGH STRAIGHT RULER handy. Straight line with a ruler can be made in half the time needed for freehand. More efficient and trustworthy.

182. Using a <u>CURVED RULER</u> is the easiest way to blend a new cutting line into the original pattern cutting line. Once you get the "hang" of it, it's so much quicker than any other sewing aid. Any part of the ruler curve can be used.

183. Grandmother used SAFETY PINS instead of a LOOP TURNER.

If neither is available, hook a LONG BOBBY PIN in a notch at one end. Slide it through tubing to the other end. PERFECT.

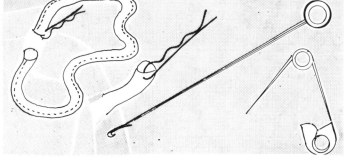

184. Use a <u>NON STRETCH TAPEMEASURE</u>. If you're using a "GIVE-AWAY," measurements may be "off." Garment may be "whopsided."

27

185. Carry a RETRACTABLE TAPEMEASURE. It comes in handy for unexpected grandchildren measurements, fabric stretch, yardage, etc.

186. Find the TAPEMEASURE in a hurry. Tape a few inches to the top front edge of your sewing machine.

187. Treat yourself to a PRIDE & JOY" SEWING BOX. I've had an expandable sewing box for years. It cost $35.00 a long time ago.

The price is forgotten long before grandchildren point with pride that it belonged to grandmother.

188. SNAP TAPE is used a lot on children's clothes.

Dritz® IS A GOOD BRAND OF SNAP TAPE TO USE

Snaps are evenly spaced on the tape.

DYE OR TINT THE TAPE TO MATCH YOUR FABRIC — SAVES LOTS OF SEWING TIME, TOO!

Use is not limited to children's clothes. Try SNAP TAPE on fabric toys and your own clothing.

189. USE A THIMBLE ... Saves your finger and keeps it from looking like a bloody pincushion.

A FILIGREED GOLD THIMBLE WITH AN OPENING ON ITS FACE FOR YOUR FINGERNAIL MAKES A LOVELY GIFT FOR YOU AND YOUR SEWING FRIENDS

190. Trace SEAMS and CUTTING LINES at the same time with a DOUBLE TRACING WHEEL MARKER. Use for marking pleats, tucks, lapped seams and topstitching. It's adjustable. Ask at the fabric shop.

191. DINNER FORK may substitute as a TRACING WHEEL.

192. A POINT TURNER will save time and frustration in getting PERFECT corners on collars, cuffs and other hard to reach areas.

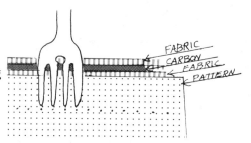

FABRIC
CARBON
FABRIC
PATTERN

BUY TWO. Have one by the sewing machine and one in the sewing box.

DO NOT use pins, scissors or other sharp objects to get your "corners." Scissors cut ... pins cause corners to sag and pull raw threads to the outside.

193. Save FINGERNAILS and use TWEEZERS to pull threads when ripping.

194. Keep a pair of "plucking" TWEEZERS handy to remove thread and large lint pieces that may have jammed bobbin operations.

195. HAVE A GOOD YARDSTICK ...

Don't let the children play "horsey" with it. Sometimes, give-aways look like someone stepped in the center. Really blows the straight line and can affect the measurements.

196. Try the inexpensive ADJUSTABLE THIMBLE. It's made from plastic with a protective "ridge" which rests UNDER THE FINGERNAIL.

Finger is protected from punctures and nail isn't broken.

CLEANING ... DYEING ...
PRETREATING ... STAINS

197. HOT WATER and TEA BAGS will dye SLIP STRAPS, SNAP TAPE or LACE. Small items can be dyed in a kitchen cup.

198. PANTYHOSE and stockings get darker when "simmered" 10 to 12 minutes in HOT WATER and TEA BAGS.

Keep in mind the number of tea bags determines darkness of the tint.

199. STAINS and SOIL will come out with less frustration if an EMBROIDERY HOOP is used to hold fabric firmly.

Working from the WRONG side, apply cleaning solution. Be sure to have a soft towel or cloth on the reverse side to catch excess cleaning solution.

200. KEEP EMBROIDERY PROJECTS CLEAN ... No matter how

clean your hands, the project picks up dirt and oil from handling.

Place embroidery on LOWER hoop ring. Place piece of white flannel over the project. Put UPPER hoop on, over the flannel.

Starting in the CENTER, cut flannel pieces ONLY toward the hoop in pie wedges. BE SURE TO CUT "PIE WEDGES" ON THE BIAS, so there's little or no ravelling.

When working on the project, flannel "pie wedges" can be folded away from the center. Hands come in contact with the flannel instead of embroidered fabric.

201. EMBROIDERY HOOPS may stain light colored fabrics. Place TISSUE PAPER on the BOTTOM hoop. Tissue paper may also be placed on top of the fabric. Tear tissue away after UPPER hoop has been applied.

202. To avoid staining fabric, BOTH EMBROIDERY HOOPS may be wrapped with white bias tape. Open up the tape and press open before wrapping each ring. DO NOT GLUE.

203. DO NOT DRYCLEAN, WASH OR IRON any fabric until stains or spots have been treated and/or removed.

204. Remove BALL POINT PEN marks with ALCOHOL. Wet a cotton ball with alcohol. Blot the mark while holding a dry cotton ball on reverse side of the fabric.

Also, ink mark should wash out if first sprayed with HAIRSPRAY.

205. DO NOT use HOT WATER, STEAM or PRESS any stains from BLOOD, EGGS or MEAT. Heat will set the stain and it may never come out.

206. To remove BLOOD STAINS, RINSE THE SPOT INSTANTLY with COLD WATER (no soap) ...OR ... moisten a ball of thread with your own saliva. Blot up the spot.

207. Remove GRASS STAIN by rubbing it with KARO SYRUP. Let it sit for 10 - 12 minutes. Wash.

208. Sometimes, GREASE STAINS will "come out in the wash" if a bottle of Coca Cola is poured in the water with detergent.

209. LIPSTICK stains will come out in the wash, if first SPRAYED with HAIRSPRAY.

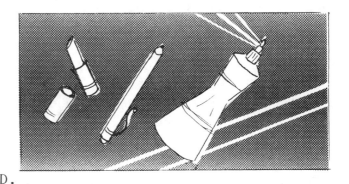

210. Sometimes, MAKE-UP stains on clothing will come out when rubbed with a slice of WHITE BREAD.

211. Remove SCORCH STAINS ... Cut an onion in half. Rub the RAW side on scorched area. Wash in cold water.

212. Remove TOMATO and some WINE stains by dousing with CLUB SODA before stain has a chance to dry. Wash.

213. Sometimes, RED WINE stains will come out if boiled in MILK.

Also, rub a little SHAVING CREAM on the stain. Wash in cold water. TEST FIRST.

214. Lift CANDLE and BEESWAX stains out. Place brown bag or paper towels on top of stain. Run a hot iron over the bag/towel.

215. Some stains can be removed by rubbing TOOTHPASTE on the area. Wash out.

216. Sometimes MARKS and STAINS can be erased from fabric with a GUM ERASER.

217. ODORS, GREASE and PERSPIRATION stains come out of SYNTHETIC fabrics if washed in IVORY SNOW.

218. Remove MUSTARD from clothing by blotting surface with a dry cloth. DO NOT try to wipe off with water.

Allow to dry. After drying, gently flex the fabric. Most of the mustard will fall out in small particles. Wash.

219. If all else fails, mix cup of <u>WARM WATER</u> with a "smidge" of <u>WHITE VINEGAR</u>. Wet the <u>stained area</u>. Keep blotting with a cotton ball or towel.

220. <u>ALWAYS WASH</u> a garment after treating for stain.

221. In a hurry and your one good outfit is wet/damp? Put a clean **WHITE BATHTOWEL** in the dryer. It helps absorb the moisture and garments will dry in less time.

222. Easy **LINT REMOVAL** from dark fabrics, velvet, corduroy, etc. Place garment on a flat surface. Rub lightly with a **damp, rough terry cloth**.

223. <u>PRESHRINK FABRIC</u> in the same manner to be used after garment is made.

224. <u>PRESHRINK FABRIC</u> immediately after purchase. Attach **CARE** instruction label with a safety pin. Make note of the yardage amount and pattern to be used on a small envelope and pin to the fabric.

Saves time to put pattern with the fabric. Put **THREAD, BUTTONS** and **ZIPPER TAB** on a double strand of **DENTAL FLOSS**. Pin to the fabric.

To really keep it all together, put pattern and notions in a ziploc food bag. Place in the fabric fold.

(Don't forget to cut a small fabric swatch to put in the **SAMPLE** notebook).

225. Are you a "HITTER" and "MISSER" at pretreating fabric? If you're one of those well organized fabri-holics who pretreats (or drycleans) fabric the moment you get home, you won't need this advice.

If you're a "hitter" and "misser" ... sometimes you do and sometimes you don't, better listen.

TAG THOSE PIECES when they come out of the DRYER (or from the cleaners) as "PRETREATED." Perhaps attaching the CARE INSTRUCTION LABEL with a safety pin will do the job. Care label says "you did it" and "how you did it."

It's really frustrating to not know what has and has not been pretreated.

226. KNOW WHAT CARE INSTRUCTION NUMBERS MEAN ... Usually, fabric cardboard core shows only the CARE INSTRUCTION number.

Care Instruction No.	Meaning
1	Machine Wash, Warm Water.
2	Machine Wash, Warm Water, Line Dry.
3	Machine Wash, Warm Water, Tumble Dry; Remove Promptly.
4	Machine Wash, Warm Water, Delicate Cycle; Tumble Dry Low; Use Cool Iron.
5	Machine Wash, Warm Water, Do Not Dry Clean.
6	Hand Wash Separately; Use Cool Iron.
7	Dry Clean Only.
8	Dry Clean; Pile Fabric Method Only.
9	Wipe with Damp Cloth Only.

227. Bought fabric off the bargain table and don't know how to pretreat it? ...OR ... lost the care instruction label and can't remember what was on the bolt end?

Squeeze the corner for a few seconds. If it bounces back without wrinkles, it's probably POLYESTER, DACRON or a combination synthetic with natural fibres.

Cut off a small scrap and hold a lighted match to it. If it chars into a small plastic ball, it's synthetic. Natural fibres like cotton, silk, etc. turn to ashes.

WOOL smells when it burns. When it's WET, it smells like a wet dog.

228. Don't forget to PRETREAT TRIM. "Disaster" is when TRIM is smaller than the garment after washing.

229. PRETREAT TRIM/TAPE without tying up yourself. Bend

the card without removing tape/trim. Leave in a container of hot water for about 10 minutes. Remove and let the tape/trim dry with the card "bent out of shape." Tape won't wrinkle and it's still on the card for easy storage.

230. If SWEATER or other fabric ravels or runs, stitch 1/4" from the edge before pretreating.

231. The manufacturer generally shrinks BLUE JEANS. You may shrink JEANS further by washing in a low level of HOT WATER. The process can be repeated several times to get them really "skin tight."

232. CLEANING MADE EASIER ...

Tape a PAPER BAG to the edge of your sewing table for clipped threads and other little "messes."

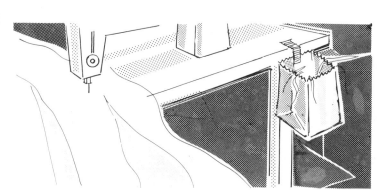

233. To pick up lint and other small threads, wrap three fingers with tape, STICKY SIDE out.

Run over the area in need of cleaning.

234. QUICK CLEANUP, if an old sheet is placed on the floor when sewing. Lift sheet and shake over the trash container.

235. Use of FUSIBLE WEB causes a residue on the iron soleplate. To keep the iron from dragging, apply cleaner and wipe off. Ask at the fabric shop about "CLEAN & GLIDE."

236. To remove BURNED STARCH from bottom of the IRON, rub with THREE TABLE SPOONS SALT sprinkled on brown paper bag.

Iron should be WARM ... not hot.

237. Remove FUSIBLE RESIDUE from iron soleplate ... Spread SALT over WAX PAPER (waxed side up).   Set

iron heat on DRY MEDIUM. Iron the salt and wax paper. Let the iron cool. Wipe off residue with damp cloth.

238. RENEW the BOTTOM of your STEAM IRON ... Dip a fine abrasive pad in AMONIA/WATER solution. Scrub gently ... OR ... rub area with a soft cloth dipped in HEATED solution of WHITE VINEGAR and SALT.

    Finish cleaning with silver polish.

239. If SCISSORS get "gummy" rub with artists' OIL PAINT THINNER. Smells good and cleans instantly.

240. NAIL POLISH REMOVER will get rid of "GOOEYS" on needles, pins, scissors, etc.

241. Clean the machine before starting to sew.

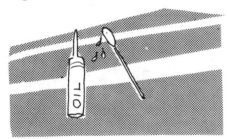

Dip Q-TIP in a little machine oil. Run it in and about the needle and bobbin area. It will pick up all kinds of lint and dust. Lubricates a little at the same time. One "swipe" with a "swab" does the "job."

242. Use a PIPE CLEANER to clean lint and dust from hard-to-reach areas of the sewing machine. It's small, long and stiff. Does a good job.

243. KEEP THE MACHINE FREE OF LINT ...

    Oil and clean it regularly. Cover, when not in use. READ THE MACHINE MANUAL.

    Regular brushes are available for cleaning lint from hard-to-reach places. The ARTIST'S PAINT BRUSH is an excellent cleaning brush, also. The handle is L-O-N-G and gets into every little crack and crevice ...AND you can see where it's going.

244. WASH AN OLD MASCARA BRUSH and use it to clean lint from the BOBBIN CASE. A Q-Tip also works well for this purpose.

245. UNFUSING FUSIBLE WEB ... Steam fused area and gently pull apart. Rub fusible residue while it is still soft from steam, with DAMP CLOTH and BAKING SODA.

If residue hardens, apply little more steam and continue to rub until all is removed.

246. Rubbing area with DENATURED ALCOHOL will also remove fusible interfacing and bonding residue.

247. Fusible residue may also be removed by placing CHEESECLOTH on the area and applying steam.

Cheesecloth will absorb residue off the fabric.

248. A "POX" may descend upon you if CANVAS handbags and belts are washed in the washing machine.

Get a cup of upholstery/carpet cleaning solution from your upholstery shop owner. He'll probably even show you how to use it.

If he's not too "friendly" buy the smallest quantity possible. Remove all earthly possessions from the bag and stuff with a dry, soft cloth to absorb the moisture ... try a terry towel.

Dampen the soiled areas and rub gently with a cloth dipped in the cleaning solution. If soil is stubborn, use a lightweight fingernail brush to scrub gently.

249. CLEANING FANCY PILLOWS ... Spray both sides with a solution of 1/2 cup PINE SMELLING CLEANER/1 CUP WATER. Place in dryer on permanent press setting for about 10 minutes.

250. CLOSE VELCRO FASTENERS BEFORE WASHING ... they last longer and will not snag other garments.

251. To keep UNDERWEAR and BLOUSES WHITE, mix a QUARTER CUP WHITE VINEGAR in the rinse water.

252. Some POLYESTERS can be brightened and whitened by soaking in a solution of 1 cup diswasher detergent and 1 gallon water.

253. To remove CHEWING GUM, try ICE ... Hold a cube on top of the gum. Gum should harden and peel off.

If gum doesn't come off, put it between two ice cubes and try again.

RUBBING THE AREA WITH CIGARETTE LIGHTER FLUID or TURPENTINE will also remove gum.

WARNING: Test first for discoloration.

254. Get "GRUNGIES" out of WHITE COTTON things by boiling with LEMON SLICES.

My mother did this in a big three-leg black pot by the creek when I was little. I was sure she wasted lemons.

255. Bleach tends to age fabrics; but do try a small amount of CLOROX mixed with DISHWASHER DETERGENT to brighten your white COTTONS.

256. A smidge (and I do mean a "SMIDGE") of BLEACH and two teaspoons WHITE VINEGAR in 1 1/2 gallons WARM WATER will take the "GRUNGIES" out of once white nylon garments.

257. DENIM will look new, LONGER if it is soaked in a mixture of WATER and WHITE VINEGAR before washing.

258. Keep LEATHER garments looking new. With a soft cloth, apply solution of one half LINSEED OIL/ONE HALF WHITE VINEGAR.

259. If garment has two or more colors that may FADE or BLEED, add SALT to the WASH WATER. Salt may prevent colors from "running."

260. If garment has been worn until it SHINES, RUB WHITE VINEGAR, FULL STRENGTH, on shiny area in all directions.

261. Wash WOOL garments in cold water and WOOLITE or
mild soap.

Don't use too many suds. Don't rub the
garment.

A capful of AMMONIA will brighten garment
colors. (Keep it away from heat).

One third cup WHITE VINEGAR in the
final rinse water will assure there are no suds left to make
colors drab.

262. WASH SWEATERS IN THE SAME MANNER AS WOOL. Soften
the garment by adding a TEASPOON of HAIR CREME
RINSE to the final rinse water.

Blot excess water with a clean terry cloth towel. Lay
it on a clean towel to dry. Use cool iron on the WRONG
side.

263. Wash SWEATERS or other garments that "PEEL" or has
"pile," WRONG SIDES OUT.

264. BLEACH ON POLYESTERS
and NYLON? ...

Polyester and nylon
"pretties" get gray
and dingy after
several washings.

It's because they pick
up color from other things
in the wash.

They still get dingy after several separate washings.

You've been told not to use bleach because it ages,
eats or turns the garment yellow. Not necessarily.

Some POLYESTERS and NYLONS can be washed with bleach
and take on a glorious new SPARKLE.

BEWARE: TEST BLEACH A FEW SCRAPS FIRST.   If it
works with scraps, use a little bleach on the garments.

265. Try the SAFETY TEST for BLEACHING ... Mix 4 tablespoons
WATER with 1 tablespoon BLEACH. Put a drop on the
garment seam allowance or scrap.

If the odor changes, better leave the bleach alone
for that particular garment.

266. Steam may cause <u>METALLIC THREAD</u> in fabric to rust and all lustre disappears.

If metallic thread rusts, wash in a mixture of **LUKE WARM WATER** and **ONE CUP WHITE VINEGAR.**

Doesn't work all the time but it's worth a try.

267. Add 1/3 cup **WHITE VINEGAR** to rinse water for <u>washable SILKS.</u> It will eliminate soap residue and prevent its turning yellow. Vinegar also keeps colors from fading.

If white vinegar is not available, add one **bottle cap AMMONIA** and **HYDROGEN PEROXIDE** to the wash water. This will also keep **WHITE SILKS** from turning yellow.

268. Keep a supply of <u>INK BLOTTERS</u> on hand.

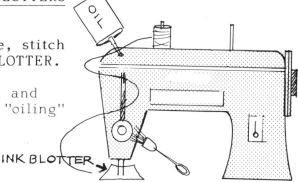

After oiling the machine, stitch several seams on the BLOTTER.

Excess oil is eliminated and there's no worry about "oiling" the garment.

INK BLOTTER➤

HELP WITH FIT & MEASUREMENTS

269. If <u>"YOU"</u> get out of the way for a minute, <u>"YOU"</u> can do a better job of deciding what looks good on <u>"YOU."</u>

Hide your head under a box or bag with holes for eyes and look at yourself in a full length mirror.

You will see yourself with a different pair of eyes and know whether you're standing straight or slumped.

This works very well when loosing weight and need to decide which areas of the body need improvement.

Use the technique to buy new clothes. All sales personnel will be sure you're "playing looney tunes" ... but then, you may never have to return a garment.

270. Have a friend take your **MEASUREMENTS.** Taking your own can result in a bad fitting garment.

Have measurements taken in underwear to be worn under clothing to be made.

Wear a good bra for bust measuring.

Record measurements on your chart in pencil. They can be changed from time to time as needed.

DON'T FORGET TO USE A TAPEMEASURE THAT DOES NOT STRETCH.

271. Measure BUSTLINE and HIPS at the FULLEST POINT.

To find center back to waistline, feel top bone at neck back. It will protrude the most when head is bent forward. Measure from bone to waistline.

272. If the difference between HIGH BUST (chest) and FULL BUST is more than 2 1/2" - 3" use the HIGH BUST measurement when choosing a pattern size.

Make full bust alteration.

273. It's easier to get correct body measurements if a CORD is tied around the WAISTLINE.

If a cord is not available and you're wondering where the waistline is, bend sideways. Slip index finger into the body "bend." That's the waistline.

274. For correct arm length, measure from shoulder edge to the WRIST, with arm bent slightly.

275. PROPER FINISHED SLEEVE LENGTH ... Hold the arm straight. Fold the palm. Longest finger should reach to the point where FINISHED sleeve edge should be.

276. For a better SHOULDER FIT, measure with elbows bent, hands clasp together. Hold hands 6" to 7" away from center of chest.

277. DRESS FORM can be indispensable to the lady who sews a lot. Choose carefully. They save little time in actual sewing but a lot of time is saved in fitting and ripping out.

Dress form should be on an adjustable stand for ease in raising and lowering.

Be sure it has collapsible shoulders and can be stuck with pins. (Collapsible shoulders allow dress or skirt with waistline/waistband over the shoulders without ripping).

278. SUBSTITUTE DRESS FORM ... Pin garment waist to a LAMPSHADE, at the point where measurement around shade is the SAME as WAIST MEASUREMENT. Pinning the HEM evenly is easy. (Be sure lampshade is sturdily mounted).

279. MAKING YOUR OWN DRESS FORM ... Put on an old T-shirt. Get a friend to wrap 1" gummed tape around the waist, down center front and back.

Then wrap horizontally until the shirt is completely covered. Use small strips around the bustline.

Cut T-shirt up the back. Remove. Retape. Shellac. When the form is dry, cover with knit tubing.

280. BE SURE TO EXAMINE FABRIC FOR FLAWS BEFORE CUTTING.

281. EASY TO CUT STRAIGHT if you look ahead to where you're going instead of where you are or where you've been.

282. QUICK way to cut EVEN STRIPS from fabric ... especially leather, vinyl, ultra suede(r) ...

TAPE
TAPE

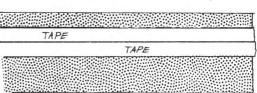

Place desired width masking tape on wrong side of the fabric. Cut **along** the tape edge.

283. CUTTING FUR or PILE FABRIC ...

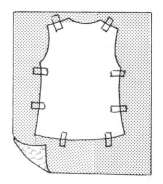

Place pattern on the WRONG side. DO NOT PIN. Use PATTERN WEIGHTS ... or TAPE pattern in place ... or MARK THE PATTERN LINE and cut.

CUT THE BACKING ONLY (not the fur or pile) with "SHORT SWIPES" in the fur/pile direction.

Before sewing, trim fur/pile away from the seam allowance with scissors tips. Lay fabric on a flat surface, WRONG side down. **TRIM AGAINST** the fur/pile on RIGHT side.

Trimming is a little easier if fabric and surface edges are flush.

284. Use "NAPPY" fabric as a pad on cutting table/board. Nap will hold fabric in place as it is being cut. Make pad in the same manner you would make a fitted sheet (to stretch over the mattress).

285. DO NOT use TRACING WHEELS and CARBON PAPER on KNITS. Tracing wheel cuts knit fabric fibres.

286. CUT ALL GARMENT PIECES ON FABRIC WITH A NAP, in the SAME DIRECTION.

287. CAMEL HAIR and CASHMERE should be cut in the NAP DIRECTION.

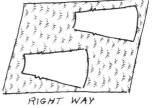

WRONG WAY   RIGHT WAY

Hold fabric up to your body. Run your hand downward. If it is smooth to the touch, that is the NAP DIRECTION.

VELVET and CORDUROY will look richer if it is cut AGAINST the nap. If fabric is ROUGH to the touch when running the hand downward, it is AGAINST THE NAP.

288. If in doubt about the direction of cutting SHINY FABRICS, cut all pieces in ONE DIRECTION. Shiny fabrics, like satin, can have a "nap" too.

289. Vinegar will NOT REMOVE PERMANENT FOLD/CREASE IN THE CENTER OF COTTON KNITS. In fact, nothing will

remove it. Cut garment pieces on the sides AWAY FROM THE CENTER.

Use center fold area for sleeves or other pieces on which the permanent fold/crease will not matter.

290. CUT GARMENT PIECES RIGHT SIDES TOGETHER (unless matching plaids or stripes).

More time can be saved by pinning in three or four locations before lifting cut pieces off the table.

291. MAKE NO MISTAKES when working with LOOK-ALIKES. Raglan sleeves seem to be the biggest culprit.

Cut out front pieces with PINKING SHEARS. Use regular SCISSORS to cut out back pieces.

292. With QUILTED FABRICS, cut ONE piece at a time. Reverse the pattern piece and cut opposite side.

DO NOT CUT ANY PIECE ON THE FOLD.

293. If a WHOLE OUTFIT (blouse, skirt, jacket, etc.) is to be made, cut out all garments at one time. This will be an incentive to finish all garments instead of making one and putting the others away until "you get to it."

If more than one garment is to be made from the same fabric, save money. Lay out all pattern pieces on fabric before purchase. You can save 1/4 to 3/4 yard, (depending on number of garments to be made) or more by relocating small pattern pieces on the fabric.

INTERFACING

294. Purchase 5 - 10 yards of INTERFACING at one time. Waste will be much less.

295. Eliminate wasted time to trim off INNTERFACING PIECES. Make PATTERN INTERFACING PIECES and place in the envelope.

296. Usually, interfacing is not necessary on "QUILTEDS." DO use a TRIM instead of facings.

297. DO NOT use FUSIBLE INTERFACINGS on lace, eyelets or other hole-ly fabrics.

298. TEST before using FUSIBLE INTERFACING on fine, sheer or silk fabrics. NUDE color voile, organza, fine mesh nylon net or self fabric works better.

299. PRESHRINKING FUSIBLE INTERFACING ... If there is any doubt as to whether you should preshrink fusible interfacing, DO IT.

Preshrink by placing in **WARM WATER** 10 to 15 minutes. **DO NOT WRING.** Gently, squeeze out excess water. Line dry.

Also, fusibles may be pretreated by steaming 10 to 12 seconds prior to permanent application with iron and pressing cloth. (Be sure fusible side is **UP** and **DO NOT TOUCH** with the iron).

300. Interfacing WRINKLES and creases CANNOT BE PRESSED OUT before use.

To avoid creases and wrinkles, accordian fold the interfacing and hang with flip-type skirt hanger.

It's also easier to see the amount of interfacing on hand.

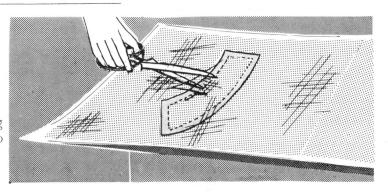

301. If possible, interfacing should be same color as the fabric.

For best results, **KNIT** fusible interfacing should be used on **KNITS** and **WOVEN** interfacing should be used on **WOVENS**.
INTERFACING SHOULD TOLERATE SAME TREATMENT AS FABRIC ON WHICH IT IS USED.

302. Save TRIMMING TIME on inter-facing pieces.

Place pattern on the bottom. Lay interfacing material on top of the pattern piece.

Cut interfacing 1/2" less than pattern piece.

303. NO "TELL-TALE" RIDGES when piecing fusible interfacing.

44

Cut both piecing ends with pinking shears. Fit "pinked" teeth to each other.

304. Cut INTERFACING on the bias. It will have more flexibility and fit better.

If fusible interfacing is undesireable, try a FABRIC GLUE to attach garment and interfacing.

Some glues dry quickly and do not wash out. Use SPARINGLY along the SEAM ALLOWANCE.

Ask at the fabric shop and test brands for preference. DO READ PACKAGE INSTRUCTIONS BEFORE USING.

305. If more than one gar- ment is to be made from the same pattern, CUT ALL INTERFACING pieces at the same time i.e. two collars, four cuffs, etc.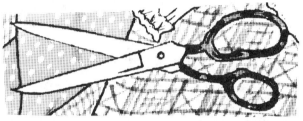

Use one set and put the other in the pattern envelope.

GOOD SCISSORS should cut through four layers of interfacing ... you've saved half the cutting time.

306. NYLON NET TULLE, BRIDAL VEILING and ORGANDY are good INTERFACINGS for SHEERS.

It gives "body" without bulk and won't show like the traditional interfacing.

BEWARE: Be sure to press with iron on a very low temperature setting.

307. Try GROSGRAIN RIBBON to INTERFACE/LINE WAISTBANDS.

Cut band one half the pattern width PLUS 5/8" (for seam allowance).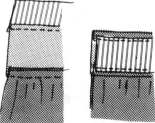

Sew band to the garment, RIGHT sides together, sew 1 1/2" wide ribbon to free edge and each end.

Turn. Slipstitch in place.

Eliminates unnecessary bulk. Works super great with wools

308. When HEMS (on Jacket Sleeves, too) require interfacing,

try the fusible kind instead of handbasting. Cut bias
strips 2" to 2 1/2" wide. It makes a nicer hem.

309. INTERFACE BOTH SIDES of
      COLLAR and CUFFS in KNIT
      garments.

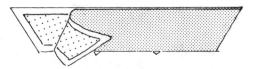

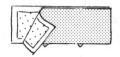

This is important to keep one side
from stretching out of shape during
construction.

310. INTERFACE pocket pieces on knit garments. Keeps them
      from sagging. Use a fusible KNIT INTERFACING.

311. Use SCRAPS of FUSIBLE INTERFACING to patch trouser
      pockets.

312. Use 1" COTTON BIAS TAPE as an INTERFACING for the
      simple, stand-up collar.

      Bias tape will conform easily to the pattern piece curve
      and has just enough stiffness to stand up.

      Add a little more "STIFF" with several rows of topstitching
      after garment is complete.

313. Extend INTERFACING a "smidge" beyond the FOLD LINE
      for a softer "ROLL" on garment center closing.

      (This is an exception to the general rule that interfacing
      should not be caught in seam allowances).

314. SECURE GARMENT FRONT/SIDE SLITS ... Where
      there are "slits," there's likely to be stress at
      seam's end.

      Sew in small squares of lightweight INTER-
      FACING with seams at "stress" points.

      Prevents the area from ripping or tearing.

PINNING

315. Pin as many garment pieces together as possible, AT
      THE SAME TIME. Then sew.

316. Use long, thin PINS with LARGE HEADS. They're easier
      to put in, see and pull out.

317. Pin garment pieces together with PIN HEADS to the

<u>OUTER EDGES.</u>   Three to ten minutes can be saved on each garment.

318.   Save PIN "putting and pulling" time. Use as few pins possible without loosing control.

Sew a pant leg, blouse, skirt or dress SIDE seam with two pins – one at each end.

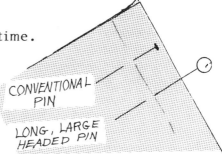

CONVENTIONAL PIN

LONG, LARGE HEADED PIN

319.   Use LOTS of PINS to apply CUFFS, sew in SLEEVES and other small areas.

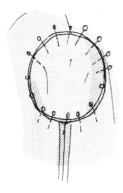

Use a pin every half inch when sewing CONCAVE to a CONVEX CURVE.

320.   If pins are likely to leave holes in the fabric, HAIR CLIPS may be used to hold lightweight fabrics together.

321.   PIN HOLES appear if pattern is pinned to LEATHER/VINYL or similar fabrics.

If pinning is absolutely necessary, do so only in the seam allowance.

322.   Instead of pinning LEATHER/VINYL, place pattern on fabric with WEIGHTS or a little TRANSPARENT TAPE.

Dust around pattern edges with chalked eraser. Lift pattern and there's a perfect cutting line.

323.   Use <u>BUTTERFLY MOUNTING PINS</u> when working with fine SILK.

They're L-O-N-G and TISSUE PAPER THIN.   Never leaves a trace of pin holes.

324.   To eliminate pins slipping out of SILKY fabrics, push in and out TWICE.

325.   To avoid pin marks on VELVETS, CORDU-ROYS, pin ONLY in the seam allowance.

326. Thought you'd handsew and watch TV?   End up with a backache?

Put a pillow in your lap. Work with your project on top. Really helps.

327. If THIMBLE is missing, wrap FINGER with TAPE ... loosely; don't cut off blood circulation.

328. Cut off 1 1/2" - 2" THUMB and NEEDLE FINGERS of an old RUBBER GLOVE.

Place on fingers for projects where it's hard to get hand needle through the fabric.   Rubber fingers grasp needle and it pulls through stubborn areas easily.

Saves fingers and speed up the project.

329. HAND WORK is a little faster if several needles are threaded at the same time before project commences.

330. Keep several NEEDLES THREADED with BLACK and WHITE thread. These are basic colors and handy for handbasting.

331. Leave HANDWORK by the telephone.   Sew on buttons, snaps and other little jobs when talking.

332. When HANDSEWING, push needle with thimble SIDE instead of the END.

Needle will go through straighter.

333. HANDSEWING THREAD tangles less if length is limited to 18" - 20."

334. BEESWAX for HANDSEWING ...

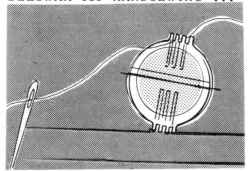

Cut thread 18" - 20" long and run through beeswax.   Thread won't knot.

BEWARE: If beeswaxed thread is used for decorative topstitch,   DO   NOT   PRESS

48

WITH HEAT. Beeswax may melt into the fabric and vinegar will not remove the little spots.

MORE WARNING: One lady left her beeswax in the car on a 109 degree day. It MELTED and her car didn't even smell like clover. Enough said.

335. It's easier to thread a hand needle if THREAD IS CUT ON AN ANGLE.

336.  Handsewing thread tangles less if KNOT END comes off the spool last.

THREAD THE NEEDLE and then cut.

337. Some sewing ladies swear THREAD WILL NOT KNOT if it's IRONED before use.

338. Another way to eliminate tangles in handsewing thread ... Without putting a knot in the thread, sew 20 – 30 stitches on laundry softner sheet.

Pull all thread out. Elim-inates static cling. Handsew with the same needle and thread.
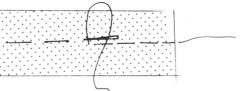

339. DOUBLE THREAD will resist tangles, if EACH END is tied with a SEPARATE KNOT.

340. HAND BASTING is not a time saver ... but ... if you insist, DO NOT KNOT the thread. It will be easier and faster to remove.

341. USE A FINE SHARP NEEDLE for HAND BASTING or there may be unsight- residual stitch marks.

342. Even BROKEN BALLOONS are USEFUL ... When handsewing through several thicknesses (quilting, topstitching blazers, etc.), it may be difficult to pull through the needle.

Hold a broken balloon between first finger and thumb. Balloon rubber grasps the needle and finger strength will surprise you. Needle pulls through with less effort.

343. Keep HAND STITCHES loose and pull gently or dimples will appear on RIGHT side of the fabric.

344. DECORATIVE HAND BASTING STITCH can be perfect ...

Machine sew a loose basting stitch next to the line on which decorative stitching is to be done.

It's easy to match HAND STITCH LENGTH with SEWING MACHINE STITCH LENGTH.

Remove machine basting after hand decorative stitch is complete.

SEWING "IT" UP

345. If things "go wrong" put sewing project aside and go back another time.

346. Do "HATE" sewing first. Everyone has a "hate" for certain little jobs. If done first, the rest will go much quicker.

347. No one will ever realize two garments are made from the same pattern if DIFFERENT FABRIC WEIGHT and TEXTURE are chosen for each.

348. It's easy to lose your place when re-arranging garment pieces at the sewing machine.

To do it right, lift presser foot but leave the NEEDLE DOWN in the fabric. Re-arrange. Lower presser foot. Sew. Seamline has not been disturbed.

349. Sometimes, weight of heavy fabric will cause SKIPPED STITCHES.

When sewing heavy or bulky items, put a chair in back of the sewing machine to support excess fabric.

350. KNOW WHAT TO DO ABOUT "SKIPPING" STITCHES ...

... Change needles; maybe the one you are using is tired.

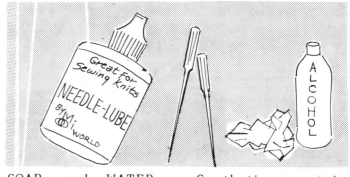

... Put a drop of Needle Lube on the Needle or WASH with SOAP and WATER. Synthetics contain a resin that builds up on the needle unless fabric is pre-treated before sewing.

... Needle may be cleaned with alcohol, also.

... Check the tension; may need to be tightened or loosened.

... Using a ROLLER FOOT might help.

... Singer's "YELLOW BAND" needle might help. It sews knits and wovens.

... Stretch the fabric slightly, as it is being sewn.

... Sew slowly (particularly on synthetics).

... Use short stitches for lightweights and long stitches for heavyweights.

... Make sure machine is correctly threaded.

... Make sure needle is properly inserted in the machine. Flat side of needle should be to flat side of machine.

... Be sure you're sewing with correct size thread for the fabric.

... Check the needle plate. You may need a "round" hole instead of "oval."

... Check the needle size. It may be too big or too small.

... Change needle to a different position – left or right. (Some machines may not have this option).

... Always use short stitches on fine, thin and sheer fabrics.

... Use a slight zigzag stitch.

... Lower the needle a "smidge." Sometimes needle is not low enough to pick up the bobbin thread.

If none of the above is causing "skipped stitches" call the friendly sewing machine repair man or buy a good machine.

351. ELIMINATE SKIPPED STITCHES caused from presser foot imbalance ...

One side of the seam area may be thicker than the other. This may be caused from seam ridges, fabric fibre, etc.

MAKE A FIXER-UPPER. Cut several strips 2" x length of a manila folder.

Cut comparable strips from 0000 EMERY CLOTH (bought in art stores).

Glue Emery Cloth to one side of the manila strip. Make several. Put your name on them. Great stocking gifts for sewing friends.

Place strip(s) where needed to even thickness under the presser foot.

Emery cloth side should be placed on top of the fabric, under the presser foot. It keeps fabric from slipping and will not snag. Manila side slides smoothly under the presser foot.

If more than one strip is necessary to even fabric thickness, strips may be stacked on top of each other.

Also, strip edge may be used as a guide for sewing straight seams.

352. To avoid MACHINE JAMMING ...

    ... Hold threads in back of the presser foot for first 4 or 5 stitches.

    ... Make sure the bobbin is threaded correctly.

    ... On some machines, needle must be in the "UP" position when sewing starts.

    ... Start sewing on a scrap in front of the garment. Sew from scrap ONTO the garment. BACKSTITCH at beginning of the garment. Clip threads holding scrap to the garment.

353. If you're RIGHT handed, it's easier to sew with GREATER amount of fabric on LEFT side of the presser foot.

354. Drill hole in a small SCREWDRIVER HANDLE. Place on the extra machine SPOOL SPINDLE or drinking straw used to extend spindle length.

Easy and quick to reach when needed.

355. To keep SLIPPERY FABRIC from sliding

off the sewing table, rest pieces on muslin, bed-sheet scrap or pillowcase.

356. Use "KEYING" system to keep small items like zipper tops, collars, etc., straight.

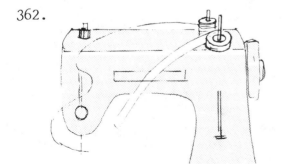

357. Re-fluff a down garment after washing. Place clean tennis shoe in the dryer with it.

358. Eliminate PUCKERS when sewing down. Use a single hole needle plate.

359. When sewing with down, if top tension is loosened a little, SKIPPED STITCHES may be eliminated.

360. Down won't creep if a WALKING FOOT is used.

361. Make a 3/4" ELASTIC BAND to fit the FREE ARM of your sewing machine. Dye it a pretty, bright color.

Put it on the FREE ARM for use as a guide in hemming, topstitching, etc.

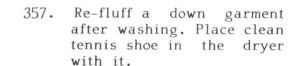

362. Place FUSIBLE WEB ROLL on the machine's second spool spindle. Sew web to garment where needed. Web will automatically unroll correctly as it is being sewn.

When finished, it takes only a second to reroll and pin end to the roll.

363. KEEP FUSIBLE WEB away from the IRONING BOARD. Scrap pieces cause "CATASTROPHE" if scrap adheres garment to the ironing board.

364. NEEDLE need not DISAPPEAR into the PINCUSHION ... Thread and knot one end. Pull thread until the knot comes in contact with needle's eye. Also keeps thread from coming out.

365. For FLATTER appearing stomach, use a SNAP instead of pant hook on skirt and pant band closures.

366. Use FASTENERS that are compatible with the garment color. Don't put black snaps, hooks & eyes and other fasteners on garments made with light color fabrics.

367. SEW A PERFECT CIRCLE in seconds ... Place tack head down on sewing machine, desired distance between tack and needle. Stabilize the tack with tape.

   Place fabric on the tack point. Sew slowly. Fabric will move in a perfect diameter.

368. Long hair gets caught and pulls in back neck hook & eye closures. Try a SIMPLE SNAP.

369. KNOW EXACTLY WHERE the SNAP "MATE" goes ... Sew on POINTED part of the snap first. Rub chalk over the point. Press into fabric on opposite side of the closure.

   Chalk mark shows exactly where MATE should be sewn.

370. Stabilize HOOKS & EYES until sewn in place ... Put a pin through the opening at each end ... try GLUE STICK for temporary "STAYING POWER."

371. Use WATER ERASABLE MARKING PENS and PENCILS for CONSTRUCTIONS MARKS.

   Tailor's tacks are too slow.

372. Use MARKING PEN or PENCIL or 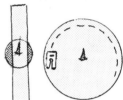 CUT NOTCHES at pattern FOLD lines.

   It only takes a "jiffy" to press in fold lines, matching up both ends.

   This also eliminates crooked fold lines.

BE SURE TO USE A MARKER THAT IS GUARANTEED "COMPLETELY REMOVEABLE IN WASHING OR DRY-CLEANING"

373. Use EMBROIDERY THREAD to make TAILOR TACKS. It's less slippery.

374. Use different color thread to make TAILOR TACKS in various areas of the garment i.e. one color for DARTS a different color for BUTTONHOLES ... a third color for POCKET PLACEMENT, TUCKS, etc.

Avoids confusion when construction marks are close together.

375. If marking pen is not available and tailor's tacks are not desireable, use PINS for CONSTRUCTION MARKS.

Push pins through the pattern and fabric at construction dots. Lift pattern off, leaving in the pins. QUICK.

376. "CLIPPING" is quicker but "NOTCHING" may be safer ... Little 1/4" clips seem to be a favorite for quick construction marks on the seam allowance.

If "clips" are missed and construction marks are not matched, garment could be a "mis-fit."

ALSO, if ripping out is necessary to adjust size, clips may no longer be a favorite. (Use marking pen instead of clips and notches ... it's quicker).

377. Most of the time, CONSTRUCTION MARKS in areas where the garment is to be interfaced can be eliminated.

Place marks on the INTERFACING instead. When garment piece is interfaced, markings are covered anyway.

378. Wipe or dust off CONSTRUCTION MARKS prior to applying heat or washing. Some detergents cause markings to "set" in the fabric.

WARNING: DO NOT use lead pencil or ball point pen to make construction marks on light color fabric, interfacing or stay. Marks may not come off and will show on the garment after completion.

Generally, lead pencil or ball point pen will not erase nor wash out.

379. Holding a STEAM IRON over TAILOR'S CHALK marks for a few seconds will make them disappear.

380. MARK the RIGHT/WRONG sides of garment pieces. Sometimes.

either side of the fabric is suitable for a garment. Use either side you wish ... but **be consistent.**

When cutting out, mark RIGHT side with a marking pen in the seam allowance. Also, TRANSPARENT TAPE may be placed on the RIGHT side of each piece.

Get in the habit of marking a PARTICULAR SIDE. There will be no confusion about which side is the RIGHT.

381. Use CONTRASTING COLOR THREAD for BASTING ... It's easy to see for quick and easy removal.

EXCEPTION: I've seen fibre residue from red thread remain in white fabric. Use light colored thread to baste light color fabric.

382. Do all BASTING at one time. Saves time changing from seam to basting stitch.

383. L-O-N-G DISTANCE MACHINE BASTING ... Always machine baste with the L-O-N-G-E-S-T stitch possible. DO NOT BACKSTITCH. Leave threads FREE at the beginning and end.

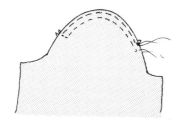

Remove basting stitches in segments. Clip the bobbin thread every few inches and pull out.

384. SHORT DISTANCE MACHINE BASTING ... For example: SLEEVE CAP.

Baste 1/8" from raw edge. PIVOT. Sew two stitches. **PIVOT** and return to original basting point. There will be only 1 set of loose thread ends.

Remove basting by clipping stitches at pivot point. Pull bobbin threads. Stitches slip out easily.

385. BASTE close to STITCHING line. When basting is removed, any marks will be almost invisible.

386. Easy GATHERING with basting stitches. ALWAYS make it a habit to baste with SPOOL thread on fabric RIGHT SIDE. Bobbin thread wil be on WRONG side.

Clip SPOOL thread close to the fabric. There's no confusion about which thread is left to PULL. Generally bobbin thread pulls easier for gathering.

56

Use BUTTONHOLE TWIST in the bobbin for basting. It's stronger for "pulling" when basting is to be removed.

387.   To hold GATHERING THREADS in place, wind ends around a straight pin several times.

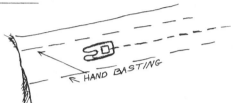

388.   <u>DO NOT</u> sew over BASTING THREADS. Sew alongside or between basting stitches.

389.   Time consuming ... but, <u>MAKES FOR EASY STITCHING ON NAPPED FABRICS</u> ...

Handbaste on each side of the seamline. Feeds through the machine easily.

← HAND BASTING

390.   INTERFACED skirt bands, cuffs, mandarin collars, pocket facings, etc. are more stable and will not stretch out of shape.

391.   Sometimes, machine will just stop, when sewing around corners. Keep a threaded needle handy to help "pull" the fabric through feed dogs.

Take a stitch right to the corner. After stitching, thread can be pulled through. Topstitched corner turns out nicely.

392.   <u>KEEP A HAT or CORSAGE PIN</u> handy at the sewing machine.

Use it to hold slippery fabrics, adjust gathers when garment is being sewn, pick out lint balls in small crevices and corners, etc.

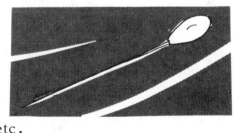

393.   SLOW DOWN on the <u>CURVES</u> and sew with SMALLER stitches. It's easier to maintain an even seam allowance.

394.   Before sewing QUILTED garment pieces together, stitch about 1/4" from all edges. Use a smaller stitch. Keeps quilting from ravelling.

395.   FACING doesn't <u>HAVE</u> to show through... If pattern calls for a COLLAR on

the garment made from sheer or fine fabric, use BIAS TAPE or STRIP instead of a facing.

396. Sew THIN and SHEER fabrics with SHORT STITCHES. Sew thick and heavy fabrics with longer stitches.

397. KEEP STITCHES FROM PULLING OUT ... Change stitch length to VERY SHORT for the first and last half inch.

   In between, sew with regular stitch length.

398. BACKSTITCHING eliminates hanging threads on finished seam ends. Start 1/2" from end of the seam. Backstitch to the fabric edges and sew toward you.

   This process helps avoid machine jam and thread knots. It also keeps finished ends, even and the garment is not "lop-sided."

399. If machine does not have BACKSTITCH capacity, stitch in place 5 or 6 times by lowering feed dogs or turning stitch control to "O" ... OR ... just hold the fabric in place with both hands.

400. Where threads must start and/or stop at an exact point (as on buttonholes, welt pockets, etc.), sew several stitches beyond the stopping point.

   Pull out extra stitches from wrong side, one by one.

   Tie off threads at the exact stopping point.

   Another way to cope with the same problem is start at the center and sew to each end.

401. ZIGZAG EDGES without ripples and curls ... Place cord or heavy string on edges of the fabric.

   Zigzag over the cord/string.
   DO NOT catch cord/string in the stitching. When zigzag is complete, pull cord or string to remove. No curls or lettuce look.

402. If SLIPPED STITCHES occur when sewing on HEAVY FABRICS like canvas or denim twill, rub SOAP EDGE along seamline.

403. To keep fabric from stretching in area to be CLIPPED, STAYSTITCH on the seamline of the single garment piece.

Be guided by pattern instructions. It may not be necessary to staystitch everything. **EXAMPLE:** Do not staystitch a bias cut skirt seamline. Do staystitch the "V" point. Curved areas on woven fabrics need to be clipped. **USE A LITTLE COMMON SENSE.**

404. STAYSTITCHING with contrasting color thread may be **easier on the eyes.** Thread is easier to see when clipping into corners or removal after sewing the garment with regular matching thread.

Do watch out for using bright color threads on light color fabrics. When removed, thread may leave unsightly fibre residual.

405. CORNERS CAN LAST as long as the garment ... Every seamstress knows how frustrating it is to make a pretty "V" neck, only to have it come out in the first wash.

Re-enforce corners with a tiny square of organdy or some other sheer, stable fabric scrap.

Use Glue Stick to center square over the POINT to which corner is being slashed.

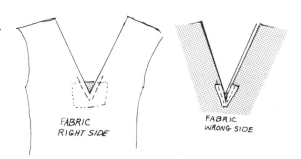

FABRIC RIGHT SIDE

FABRIC WRONG SIDE

Generally, the pattern will have slashing point marked with a dot.

Sew square to garment in the seamline, about 1/2" - 3/4" on each side. Sew two stitches across the exact corner or "point" area.

Carefully, cut into the "point" with sharp scissors. Trim scrap square to about 1/2".

Sew facing to garment (or companion garment) piece. Be sure re-enforced garment piece is on top. Pivot in the corner/point.

Corner/point will hold better if small stitches are used on each side. Regular stitches can be used thereafter.

406. EASY FLY ... Make a template from muslin. Place

template on top of the zipper area. Mark the stitching line with marking pencil or soap. Remove template and TOPSTITCH.

Also, template may be pinned in place. Use ZIPPER FOOT to stitch around the template. (Pin lightly to avoid any "pull" that may cause uneven stitching line).

407. Save $$$ on fabric for <u>LARGER SIZE PANTS</u> ... If pants cannot be made from one fabric length, consider piecing the CROTCH AREA.

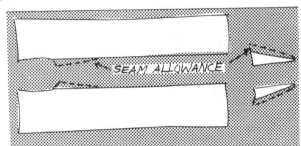

Be sure seam allowance is added to PIECINGS and PANTS LEG areas to which they are to be sewn.

408. Put on POCKETS, install ZIPPERS, TABS, COLLARS, and SEW DARTS, before sewing garment side seams.

409. <u>MAKE A NEAT TIE BELT</u> ...

Cut a piece of belting about 2" less than waist measurement.

Cut fabric piece 5/8" wider and 1" longer than belting. Sew fabric length, right sides together, using 1/4" seam allowance. Turn and press. Insert belting.

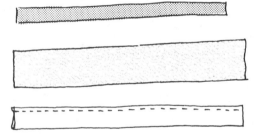

Make small ties, the length of your choice. Turn belt ends to the inside. Insert small ties in the center on each end. Sew.

410. For professional looking BELT LOOPS, ZIGZAG over a piece of <u>ELASTIC THREAD</u>.

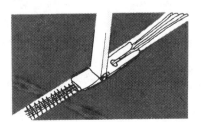

<u>OR</u> ... Use 3 to 6 strands of thread, long enough to make ALL LOOPS NEEDED. (BUTTONHOLE TWIST WORKS GREAT). Center under

the presser foot.   ZIGZAG over all thread strands.

411. If you worry about making <u>THREAD BELT LOOPS</u> without fabric underneath, place <u>TISSUE PAPER</u> under the thread. Tear away after belt loops are made.

412. BELT LOOPS will last longer if thread strands are run through BEESWAX before zigzagging.

413. <u>EASY, LESS BULKY FABRIC BELT LOOPS</u> ... Cut LENGTH 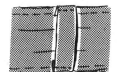 for belt loops on the SELVAGE.   Fold WIDTH in thirds. Selvage edge is on top. Press. Sew on selvage and fold edges.

Cut strip into desired belt loop lengths. Sew loops onto garment so selvage edge is next to garment and does not show.

414. Sew in BELT LOOPS between seams, BACKSTITCHING over the area for placement security.

415. End of a BUSTLINE DART should point directly to, but NOT touch, the BUST HIGH POINT. Be guided by the following:

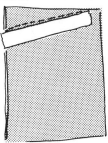

CUP SIZE	DART ENDS
A	1" away from bust high point.
B & C	1 1/2" away from bust high point.
D & LARGER	2" away from bust high point.

416. CROOKED DARTS LOOK PRETTY AWFUL ... Place edge of transparent tape alongside the dart stitching line.

Stitch alongside the tape and remove.

417. ELIMINATE BUBBLES AT DART ENDS.

Sew from dart CENTER to each end. <u>DO NOT BACKSTITCH.</u> Tie off threads.

418. MORE SECURE DARTS ... Sew darts from largest end toward the tip.

Continue sewing off the

tip until thread chain is 3/4". Raise presser foot
and bring fabric toward you. **Sew several stitches**
in the width of FINISHED DART END.

419. <u>DARTS ON HEAVY FABRIC should be</u>
<u>slashed and pressed open</u> ...

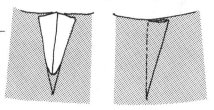

Darts on sheers may be pressed to
one side.

420. With HEAVIER FABRICS, <u>DART</u>
<u>POINTS</u> may be very stubborn about blending into the gar-
ment body.

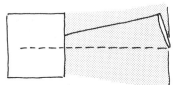

You've probably been taught to split
and press open the dart. With heavy
fabrics, the dart point cannot be split
and it "glares" back.

Pin a 2" square of lighter weight
fabric under the dart. Stitch the dart
catching 2" square.

Slit the dart. Press dart point to one
side and fabric square to the opposite side. Trim
and grade the square. DART END will blend into the
garment body nicely.

421. <u>MAKE THE DART LAY FLATTER</u> ...
Sew side seam up to the dart. STOP.
BACKSTITCH.

(DO NOT SEW ACROSS THE DART).

Lift presser foot. Push dart away
from you.

Start sewing on other side of the
dart.

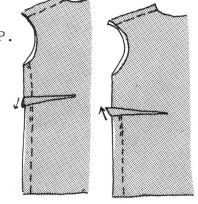

422. DARTS in a LINING should be pressed
in the opposite direction from garment
darts.

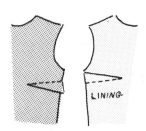

423. BUST DARTS <u>may be ELIMINATED</u> to
make more room without altering.

Baste and gather fabric edge where
dart is marked.

Sew side seams. Remove basting stitches. Trim seam
allowance to 3/8" in dart area only.

PRESS well with steam. All
visible dart signs should be gone.

424. CASINGS can hardly be felt when
garment is worn, if **hem lace,
nylon seam or bias binding** is
used.

425. Use **TWEEZERS** to run elastic or
drawstring through casing. Clamp
tweezer ends tightly over one end.

Put a rubber band over tweezer
ends, tight enough to hold elastic/drawstring in
place. Insert opposite **TWEEZER ENDS** into the casing.

426. 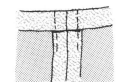 There's no need to
suffer the frustration of
having elastic caught in
casing seam allowance.

Before sewing, machine
BASTE seam allowances down in the casing area. Stitch
casing. Insert elastic. Remove basting stitches.

427. <u>EVEN and EASY APPLICATION</u> of ELASTIC
<u>or CASINGS in the WAISTLINE</u> ...

When cutting the pattern, **MARK** or **NOTCH**
the waistline on each side of FRONT and
BACK GARMENT pieces.

Measure down 2" and mark/notch again.
Elastic or casing is to be sewn on the
second marked line. (The 2" difference
provides for needed ease).

It's easier if a yardstick is used to
mark the elastic/casing application line from notch
to notch with a marking pen.

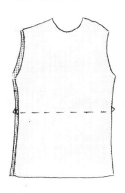  Also, FOLD may be pressed in
garment piece on the elastic/
casing application line.

Follow the marked or creased
line to sew on elastic/casing.

*Do use a STEAMSTRESS to avoid permanent
creasing; although it may not show after
elastic/casing is sewn in.

Since elastic pulls in the waist and shortens the garment, be sure to add EXTRA length when cutting.

428. CORRECT WAY TO SEW ELASTIC ENDS TOGETHER ... WILL HOLD FOREVER ...

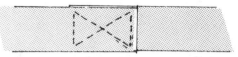

Overlap one end 3/4" on the other. Sew an HOURGLASS on the overlap. Backstitch at beginning and end.

429. QUICK REPLACEMENT OF CASING ELASTIC ...

Pull out old elastic end about 1/2".

Safety pin end of the new elastic to end of the old.

Pull opposite end of the old elastic until it has been completely replaced by the new.

430. ELASTIC APPLICATION IN KNIT (pull on) PANTS ...

Sew ELASTIC ends together. (See Tip No. 428 above). Divide into quarters and mark quarter points.

Divide Pant Waist EDGE into quarters and mark. Generally, SIDE and FRONT/BACK seams will be natural quarter points.

Matching quarter points, PIN and SEW ELASTIC and PANTS (WRONG side) UPPER EDGES. Use a Zigzag stitch and S-T-R-E-T-C-H ELASTIC even with pants edge when sewing. (Elastic will be smaller than pants).

Fold pants waist down ONE time. Elastic will be sandwiched between two layers of pant fabric. Zigzag in same stitching previously used, stretching as before.

431. SHIRRING WITH ELASTIC THREAD ... Put ELASTIC THREAD in the BOBBIN.

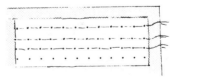

Place a strip of DOTTED PAPER on RIGHT side of the fabric area to be shirred.

Sew, using dots on the paper as guidelines. Remove paper.

432. Unless sewn correctly, ELASTIC MAY NOT RECOVER IN

64

BATHING SUITS ... I once spent hours making a bathing suit. Used the exact amount of elastic and sewed it in each leg opening as instructed. Each leg was 1 1/2" too big.

This need not happen if you have a standard method for all patterns. The usual method is to stretch elastic to the leg opening lower edge and zigzag. DON'T.

Evenly gather lower fabric edge to the ELASTIC SIZE. QUARTER ELASTIC.   QUARTER GATHERED LEG OPENING.

Then, ZIGZAG ELASTIC to the GATHERED LOWER EDGE OF EACH LEG OPENING.

When the elastic is pulled, gathering threads will break and elastic has not been stretched beyond the point of "no return."

STRETCH/PULL the elastic 3" to 4" at a time ... NEVER STRETCH THE WHOLE LENGTH AT ONCE.

Pick out gathering threads with tweezers.

433. GAUZE BANDAGES may be used in different widths for FACINGS.

434. Trim inside FACING EDGES of ARMS and NECK with PINKING SHEARS.

Hems in these areas make ridges and garment will look homemade.

Pinking is not necessary on knit fabrics.

435. SECURE FACINGS ... PRESS and PIN FACINGS IN PLACE AT THE SHOULDER SEAMS.

Stitch-in-the-ditch on the garment RIGHT side. Stitching will catch facing on the UNDER side ... OR ...

PRESS in a small piece of FUSIBLE WEB between facing and garment at the shoulder seam allowance.

436. When applying FRAY CHECK to a long edge, place garment on an empty fabric core or piece of cardboard. Cardboard will absorb excess fluid.

TRY FRAY STOP. It sprays; cardboard isn't necessary.

437. For GATHERS, baste from SIDES TO THE CENTER. There's less chance of the thread breaking. It's easier to pull two shorter threads from each side, than one long one.

438. Use FISH LINE or DENTAL FLOSS/TAPE as GATHERING CORD.

439. Pulling BOBBIN and SPOOL THREAD simultaneously will hold gathering threads in place.

440. DON'T EVER STRETCH LACE when sewing. Treat it with TLC and hold with a gentle hand.

441. DO NOT PUT BUTTONHOLE TWIST IN THE BOBBIN (except for gathering). It's too coarse for regular sewing.

442. DO NOT USE BUTTONHOLE TWIST ON SILK or FINE FABRICS at at any time.

443. Save ravelled threads from KNIT BANDS and FABRICS as well as a scrap from each garment for later MENDING.

444. If you haven't sewn for several days and forgotten what size and kind of needle is in the machine, LIFE IS HARD ... but you can fix it for next time.

Before leaving the machine, write NEEDLE SIZE & KIND on a slip of paper. Tape on the sewing machine or pin to the bulletin board ... OR ...

Leave small GARMENT SCRAP under the needle.

445. Making TINY STRAPS with a cord is easy. Cut a biased or horizontal strip 2" - 3" wide.

Use 2" or 3" LONGER than TWICE the length of straps needed.

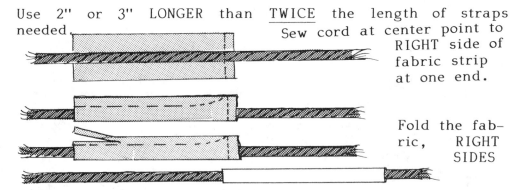

Sew cord at center point to RIGHT side of fabric strip at one end.

Fold the fabric, RIGHT SIDES together. Cord will be inside the folded fabric.

With ZIPPER FOOT, SEW at a WIDE ANGLE about 1" from the top. Sew remaining strap alongside the cord. DO

NOT CATCH THE CORD IN STITCHING. Trim the seam allowance to 1/4". PULL THE CORD GENTLY.

Strap will turn, encasing other end of the cord. Cut off cord.

446. To make QUICK TIES, STRAPS or DRAWSTRINGS, fold BIAS TAPE WIDTH and sew edges together.

447. ALWAYS place WIDEST side of BIAS TAPE on the BOTTOM.

Looking at bias tape carefully, you will see it is folded one side wider than the other.

Stitches on smaller (top side) will catch wider side on the bottom.

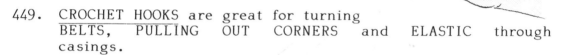

448. ERASER END of a PENCIL may be used to turn short TUB- ING, BELTING, STRAPS, etc.

THUMB and MIDDLE FINGER may be used to turn wider, shorter pieces.

449. CROCHET HOOKS are great for turning BELTS, PULLING OUT CORNERS and ELASTIC through casings.

450. QUICK WAY TO TURN SMALL STRIPS FROM FINE OR SHEER FABRICS ...

Thread large blunt end of a tapestry needle with yarn that will not break in the process. Take one or two stitches in the seam at one end of the strap.

Run the threaded needle through strap and pull - gently.

451. Turn TINY LOOPS without a loop turner. Leave bobbin and spool threads EXTRA LONG after stitching.

Trim seams close as possible to stitching. Put BOBBIN and SPOOL THREADS in a large blunt end needle. Insert needle in the loop and pull gently.

452. Instead of sewing and turning narrow straps, EDGESTITCH.

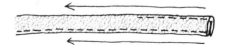

Fold strap piece in half. Press seam allowance to the inside. Stitch edges on each side IN THE SAME DIRECTION.

453. EXTRA FABRIC FORMULA for MATCHING PLAIDS ... Best way is PATTERN LAY-OUT on the fabric before purchase.

Some fabric shops will accommodate ... but ... DON'T DO IT ON A SALE DAY. Even the friendly fabric shop will turn an EVIL EYE on you for tieing up their cutting space on a sale day.

If there's no time to lay out the pattern ... or you're getting the "evil eye" from shop personnel, try "the formula."

... Measure the PATTERN REPEAT (point from where fabric pattern starts over).
... Count the number of MAJOR pattern pieces (do not count cuffs, collar, pocket, belt).
... Multiply PATTERN REPEAT MEASUREMENT times NUMBER OF MAJOR PIECES. Result is amount of EXTRA FABRIC NEEDED.
... Add amount of extra yardage to amount specified on pattern envelope for TOTAL FABRIC NEEDED.

EXAMPLE: Major pattern pieces   4
            TIMES inches in PATTERN REPEAT 6"

            Extra fabric needed .... 24"
            PLUS pattern specified yardage 2 yds.

            TOTAL NEEDED .... 2 yds., 24"
                                 (2 2/3 yds.)

454. QUICK WAY TO MATCH PLAIDS ...

Cut a single pattern piece. Turn cut piece OVER and use it as a pattern for the opposite side.

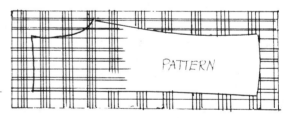

455. You may also trace PLAID FABRIC DESIGN onto the garment pattern piece.

Then, lay pattern piece on the fabric.

456. MATCH PLAIDS at the seam lines ... NOT at cutting lines.

457. If SLEEVES are cut so plaids cannot match at both front and back, MATCH AT THE FRONT.

DID YOU KNOW ...

The NEEDLE is about 30,000 years old. SAFETY PINS are only 135 years old.

458. Plaids may not match at the shoulders. It's easier to match plaids at SIDE SEAMS if there are matching problems elsewhere.

459. If garment has WELT POCKETS with FLAPS, it's easier to match plaids if flap is cut after pocket opening has been made.

460. SAVE TIME WORKING WITH PLAIDS. Cut FACINGS, POCKETS, COLLARS or other decorative pieces on the BIAS. It's different and looks nice.

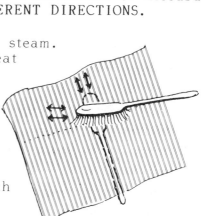

461. MATCH STRIPES (and some PLAIDS) the easy way.

Choose most predominant stripe in the fabric.

Lay ARMSCYE of both sleeves and body pattern pieces on the SAME STRIPE.

(Does not work if garment has darts).

FOR STRAIGHT HEM, cut along stripe at LOWER EDGE of the PATTERN.

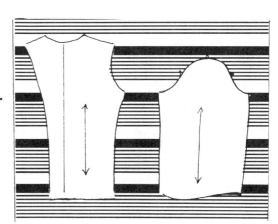

462. FIX UGLY MARKS on RIPPED OUT VELOUR or CORDUROY. On the RIGHT side, brush marks with FINGERNAIL or discarded TOOTHBRUSH. Brush in ALL DIFFERENT DIRECTIONS.

PRESS on the WRONG SIDE with steam. Brush the right side again. Repeat until the marks disappear.

463. Always use a SLIPPERY, LIGHT-WEIGHT fabric to LINE JACKETS, COATS ...

A rough textured lining causes friction with other garments, which makes it uncomfortable and frustrating to remove jacket or coat.

464. SEWING WITH FAKE FUR ... Pin pieces together. Sew with a L-O-N-G stitch. Use a SMALL seam allowance (1/4").

Place index finger between pieces in front of the presser foot. Push fur to the inside as it is being sewn. Seam will be hard to find. If fur is caught in the seam, carefully pick it to the outside with a hat pin, knitting needle or crochet hook.

465. DO NOT let SWEATER FABRIC hang over the table or ironing board when sewing or steaming.

466. Roll half used packages of SEAM BINDING, HEM LACE, TAPE, etc. around two fingers. Slide off and pin.

It's easy to see what's on hand and stays neat in the sewing basket.

467. SEWING EYELETS, LACE, NOVELTY MESHES and OPEN WEAVES can be a real "pain" and eye strainer.

... When cutting out, hold pattern pieces in place with weights. Pins will not catch in the eyelet holes.
... To transfer pattern construction marks, put pieces of tape on the fabric. Pencil mark on the tape.
... Sew French or Doublestitched seams. Make narrow, topstitched hems.
... If lace insertions are desired, topstitch lace to RIGHT SIDE of the garment. Cut fabric away from the WRONG side, leaving 1/4" seam allowance. Press seam allowances away from the lace. Sew a second time close to the first stitching. Seam allowance will lay flat.
... If underlining is needed, use a very lightweight flesh tone fabric. Batiste works well. Cut underlining from same pattern used for the garment. Stitch lining and garment pieces together.

468. Sometimes, a little TISSUE PAPER OVER or UNDER LACE can eliminate stitching problems.

469. Complete all ALTERATIONS on LEATHER-like fabrics before sewing. Ripped out stitch marks will show.

470. When sewing LEATHER-like fabrics, use TRANSPARENT TAPE or PAPER CLIPS to hold garment pieces together.

471. Apply small amount of BABY OIL with a Q-TIP on stitching area of VINYL or SMOOTH LEATHER-like fabrics.

Presser foot will move without drag.

Wipe oiled area with a clean, dry cloth after sewing.

472. For garments made from "BULKIES" use

lighter weight fabrics to make UNDER COLLARS, FACINGS, UNDER POCKET FLAPS, etc.

473. Lower FEED DOGS to remove bulky fabrics from the machine. Avoids feed dog teeth snags.

474. Keep a roll of ADDING MACHINE TAPE handy for paper when needed between feed dogs and fabric.

Put the roll on machine's second spool spindle or in a box on the floor. It rolls off easily. When project is complete, re-roll unused portion and secure with tape.

475. If feed dogs will not drop for removal of fabric, place a 3" x 5" CARD or small piece of WAX PAPER between FABRIC and feed dogs. Pull fabric over the card/wax paper and out of the machine.

476. Use the INVISIBLE ZIPPER FOOT to make PIPING. It will fit over the piping filler just like it fits over a zipper. The seam is sewn closer to the filler and straighter than with the regular zipper foot.

477. MAKE YOUR OWN PIPING ... Buy single fold BIAS TAPE.

Press open and apply piping filler.

Fold bias tape WRONG sides together with filler sandwiched between in the center.

Sew together alongside the the piping filler with ZIPPER FOOT.

478. If it's frustrating to use regular cording for piping projects, try 4-PLY YARN.

It's pliable and goes around corners. It may be stashed already in a "secret" sewing drawer. Be sure it doesn't shrink or fade in the wash after piping is made.

479. "Round" off points before applying piping, ruffles, trim or tape.

480. TRIM, PIPING, TAPE, etc. can be sewn on curves more easily if first steamed IN A CURVE on the IRONING BOARD.

481. When sewing BIAS TAPE, TRIM or PIPING

on a CONCAVE area, better S-T-R-E-T-C-H it a little, around the curve ... OR ... you'll get "fallout," (Trim, tape, etc. will be too big for the curve).

When applying trim, tape or piping on a CONVEX area, better EASE it in around the curve, or you'll get puckers.

482. PIECING BIAS or STRAIGHT STRIPS ... Place FIRST strip, WRONG side DOWN on a flat surface.

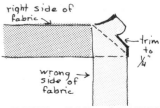

Place END and SIDE edge of SECOND strip RIGHT SIDE DOWN, FLUSH with SIDE and END edge of FIRST strip. Right sides of both strips are together.

right side of fabric

trim to 1/4"

wrong side of fabric

Looking down at the strips, sew from LEFT TOP CORNER to LOWER RIGHT CORNER.

Trim seam allowance of the UPPER RIGHT corner to 1/4". Press seam allowance open.

When applied to the garment, strip piecing is hardly visible.

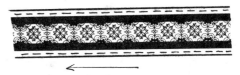

483. Sew BOTH SIDES of RIBBON, LACE, or TRIM in the same direction.

Use GLUE STICK to position.

This will eliminate twisting.

484. The PROFESSIONALS sew on GROSGRAIN RIBBON and TRIMS with a very fine zigzag stitch. Stitching hardly shows and keeps all trims even and secure. It also eliminates the frustration of "edge curls" and gaps.

485. SIMPLE THREAD ... EXTRAORDINARY TRIM ...

Topstitch area to be trimmed with a basting stitch. Thread tapestry needle with Embroidery Thread. Run needle over and under each basting stitch.

Pull the thread so it is even but not tight enough to cause puckers. (DO NOT CATCH FABRIC WITH THE NEEDLE). (Thread colors may be combined to get a different look. Makes a fascinating "rope" effect).

486.. MAKING CORDED PIN TUCKS ...

STRAW

PEARL COTTON

Cut 1 1/4" from a drinking straw.

Thread PEARL COTTON through the straw.

Insert a DOUBLE NEEDLE in the machine.
(Needle prongs should fit over the straw).

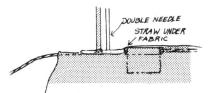

Tape straw to machine, in front of the double needle. Be sure straw does not cover needle plate hole.

Place fabric RIGHT side UP, on top of the straw. Sew.

Try on a scrap first to see the beautiful effects.

Different size straws, cord or yarn may be used. Just try it.

487. To sew on RICKRACK without frustration, place a strip of WAX PAPER on top. Sew through paper and rickrack. Tear off wax paper.

488. PLEAT SECURITY ... Sew a woven fabric square on the garment underside at the same time last 1" of pleat is being stitched.

Pleat is re-enforced and doesn't rip out when "soaring" over a mud puddle.

489. To keep a PLEAT RAZOR SHARP, press a small 1/4" strip of FUSIBLE WEB on the inside, flush with each pleat fold.

490. THERE ARE SEVERAL WAYS TO RIP OUT ...

... There's the SEAM RIPPER. It's dangerous because it does not discriminate between thread nor garment.

... Some use an they X-ACTO KNIFE but are very sharp and less caring where they cut, than the seam ripper.

Both leave behind a lot of cut threads.

The best way to remove machine stitches is to CLIP top and bottom threads EVERY INCH. Remove TOP THREAD. (Tweezers help).

On occasion, I have clipped and removed TOP THREAD only every two or three inches. Then I turn the fabric over and pull out the bottom thread. BE CAREFUL; this method can damage the fibres of silk and finer fabrics.

The CHAIN STITCH is a real "bear" to remove if you don't know where to look. To ravel, find thread on the under-side that can be pulled from LEFT to RIGHT. The bottom thread will ravel out with ease.

To ravel the BLINDSTITCH, merely pull the TOP STRAIGHT part of thread. It ravels LEFT to RIGHT.

491. After RIPPING OUT, remove thread ends residual by rubbing ripped area with PENCIL ERASER.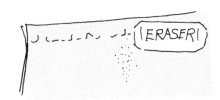

Also, a SOFT FINGERNAIL BRUSH, OLD TOOTHBRUSH or NYLON NET BALL may be used.

492. For easy RIPPING on DARK FABRICS, run CHALK lightly over stitching. Easy to see for quick removal.

493. RIPPING OUT ZIGZAG STITCHES ... You really know the mean-ing of "terror" and frustration when a "zigzag must be rip-ped.

On WRONG SIDE of the fabric, run seam ripper just under the thread (instead of between seam and fabric).

Seam Ripper will cut top layer of stitches only. Seam will separate but you'll really need the pencil eraser to remove a lot of thread ends.

494. More FULLNESS is required for RUFFLES cut from sheer or fine fabrics. 3 to 3 1/2 times actual measurement can be used.

Go easy on the amount cut from HEAVY FABRICS; limit to 1 1/2 times the actual length needed.

495. CIRCULAR or BIAS cut RUFFLES are softer and will hang more graceful.

496. EASY RUFFLES ... Baste zigzag over cording along ruffle edge. Pull the cord.

When pulled, cord doesn't break like basting stitches.

497. To make RUFFLES from SHEER/FINE FABRICS ONLY, cut fabric DOUBLE WIDTH of the pattern.

Fold ruffle LENGTH, WRONG SIDES TOGETHER. Gather CUT EDGES. No need for time consuming, handrolled edge on the outside. UPPER and UNDER RUFFLE are RIGHT sides out.

498. To find ROLL LINE on a JACKET, try it on after shoulder and side seams are sewn.

Pin front where buttons are to be placed. Roll line will be apparent from first button location to the under collar.

499. <u>USE THE SELVAGE on WOVENS</u> ...

Place straight edge of pattern on the selvage. Selvage is an automatic seam finish.

500. Cut off fabric selvages before using for patchwork pieces. Selvages are woven tighter and make it more difficult to cut pieces accurately.

501. <u>COVER SHOULDER PADS</u> ... Use nude or flesh tone fabric if pads are to be used in sheer garments.

Lay pad on WRONG side of a 12" - 14" fabric square.

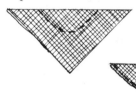

Fold fabric in a triangle over the pad.

Stitch or zigzag on round side of the pad.

Trim off excess fabric. **Don't be afraid to peel away one or two layers of a purchased shoulder pad to reduce size if necessary.

502. WHICH end of the SHOULDER PAD goes in FRONT? ... LARGER end goes in FRONT.

Just remember there's a slight "hollow" in FRONT just under the shoulder. BIG END FILLS UP THE "HOLLOW".

SMOOTH side of the pad should be next to the garment inside. EDGE should be <u>EVEN</u> with the final SEAM ALLOWANCE EDGE.

503. Shoulder pads may be moved from garment to garment. Sew self gripping fasteners on garment and pads. (Two sets of fasteners are needed for each shoulder pad).

504. <u>ADD or SUBTRACT SHOULDER PADS</u> ...

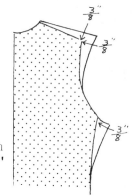

Shoulder pads may be purchased or made and there are some that may be ironed in.

If garment is to be washed, make or buy WASHABLE pads.

To put shoulder pads in a garment for which there is no provision in the pattern ADD 3/8" to UNDER ARMSCYE. ALSO, ADD 3/8" to the SHOULDER WIDTH and HEIGHT of the armhole opening.

If shoulder pads are to be ELIMINATED from a pattern for which provision HAS been made, TRIM 3/8" from BODY UNDER ARMSCYE. ALSO, TRIM 3/8" FROM SHOULDER WIDTH and HEIGHT of the armhole opening.

Machine baste sew-in-type pad to armhole SEAM ALLOWANCE (easy to remove if necessary). Tack opposite edge of the pad to shoulder seam allowance.

Generally, purchased shoulder pads have instructions. Read and follow.

505. <u>EASY SLEEVE EASE</u> ...

BASTE stitch SLEEVE CAP while holding fabric firmly against BACK of the presser foot with the left hand.

Sleeve cap should gather without pulling the bobbin threads, just enough to be eased into the armhole.

506. SLEEVE CAP CENTER should be marked or notched ... even if it's not on the pattern.

It's easier to match cap center with the shoulder seam.

507. BETTER SLEEVE FIT ... Position sleeve seam 1/4" - 3/8" IN FRONT of the garment SIDE SEAM. Sew in sleeve.

508. The <u>EASY way to sew a SLEEVE in an ARMHOLE</u> ...

... Baste 1/4" from the edge, from underarm to

to underarm on the SLEEVE. Do the same thing around the GARMENT ARMHOLE.

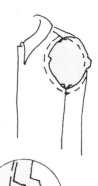

... Remark NOTCHES and CONSTRUCTION marks on sleeve and garment.

... TRIM off 1/4" from sleeve and garment armholes, using basting stitches as a guide.

With most machines, 1/4" will be automatic if side of the presser foot is kept even with fabric edge.

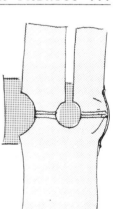

... Ease stitch 3/8" from trimmed edge from SINGLE NOTCH to DOUBLE NOTCH on the sleeve.

... Baste SLEEVE into the garment. If it is satisfactory, do FINAL SEWING.

DO NOT PRESS the SLEEVE. Press only the SEAM ALLOWANCE.

509. QUICK SLEEVE SEW-IN WITH KNITS AND STRETCH FABRICS ...

Mark center of the sleeve cap. Pin sleeve cap center to the garment shoulder seam.

Pin EACH side of the SLEEVE and GARMENT together at ARMSCYE.

With sleeve on the BOTTOM, sew. Stretch garment armhole edge even with sleeve edge, as garment is being sewn.

Sew garment side seams, starting at the bottom and out to sleeve's end.

510. The SLEEVE should have enough EASE to allow free arm movement.

Set-in sleeve seam should be no more than 1" below the armpit.

If the seam is any lower, movement of the arm will be restricted. The garment will also pull up on the sides when arm is lifted.

1"

511. Ease out unwanted sleeve darts in the same manner used for bust darts in Tip 423.

512. MITRE the PLACKET in SHIRT SLEEVES. Placket pieces will stay secure to the inside when cuff is buttoned.

513. Place LONG EYE from hook & eye combination, across bottom of a seam of any garment with a slit.

Slit won't rip because "eye" bears any seam stress.

514. With jackets and coats made from heavy fabrics, sometimes FRONT FACINGS refuse to lay flat and lapels don't turn on the "roll" line.

Turn free edge of the facing BACK about 1" and hand catchstitch it to the INTER-FACING. Start about 2" above the hem and end 2" below the shoulder.

515. Trying to put a ZIPPER in a BIAS CUT garment is like trying to teach the cat to swim. Cut two strips of fusible interfacing, width of the seam allowance by length of the zipper.

Bond to wrong side of the fabric seam allowance where zipper is to be sewn. Insert zipper.

516. BASTING TAPE may be FASTER ...

It has adhesive on both sides for FAST zipper installation, placement of tapes and trims, matching stripes, plaids and cross seams.

After use, BE SURE TO RETURN TAPE to its original package ... unless you want to stick together every notion in the sewing box.

517. If sewing bird is not available, MACHINE NEEDLE can be used as a THIRD HAND.

Place project under presser foot. Lower needle into the fabric. Hold project with one hand; sew with the other.

518. Put a CARE INSTRUCTION LABEL in the garment. Some shops will give one with fabric purchase.

519. SEW ALL STRAIGHT SEAMS at one time

520. For STRAIGHTER SEAMS, mark the machine throat plate with MASKING TAPE ... OR ... use a seam guide.

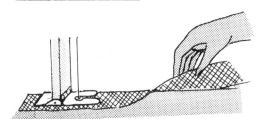

MASKING TAPE

521. FINISHED SEAMS ...

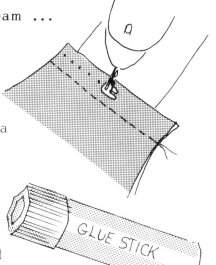

Application of SEAMS GREAT will keep edges from fraying.

It's about 5/8" wide. Comes in 10 yard rolls. There are lots of colors.

When stretched, it curls over raw edges and stitching is easy. Ask at the fabric shop.

522. NEVER sew across an unfinished seam ...

523. If it's necessary to mark seam lines to aid in trimming away excess, STITCH WITHOUT THREAD in the needle.

Little hole marks may be used as a trimming guide.

524. SEWING CURLED SEAMS ...

Spray a little STARCH on the edges and press ... OR

GLUE STICK the seams together and sew ... OR

Stitch each garment piece 1/4" from the edges and sew pieces together.

Saves "pin-pulling" time.

525. Every BIAS "has its place" ... If sewing with two layers of fabric (one cut with the grain and one on the bias), put BIAS layer on TOP when sewing BY HAND.

Put BIAS LAYER on the BOTTOM when machine sewing. It does make a difference.

526. Cut WIDER SEAM ALLOWANCES for bias garments. Patterns do not always provide. Bias seam allowances should be 1 1/2".

Bias seams grow longer and shrink in width.

527. BASTE BIAS SEAMS before sewing. Let hang for 24 hours before sewing.

Compare with the pattern to see if adjustments are necessary before sewing.

528. Use SMALLER than normal stitches to sew BIAS SEAMS.

529. Sew BIAS SEAMS with polyester or polyester/cotton thread. It has more "give" than 100% cotton thread.

530. If seams stretch when sewing BIAS SEAMS, stabilize by sewing over tissue paper. Tear paper away after sewing.

531. Sometimes the PRESSER FOOT will refuse to climb from FLAT to BULKY SEAM ALLOWANCE.

Presser Foot will be less stubborn if a small folded piece of fabric is placed under the REAR to equalize thickness of the bulky area.

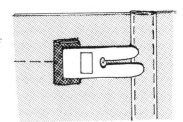

532. ELIMINATE CROOKED SEAM with napped fabrics like velour, velvet, etc.

Slip scissors points between the pieces in front of fabric as it is being sewn. Keeps seams from twisting and locking.

533. Clipping on curves weakens holding power of a seam.

Helps a little to "STAGGER CLIPS" on each SEAM ALLOWANCE LAYER.

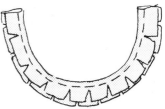

534. 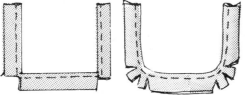 Clip PIPING or CORDING seam allowance when sewing around corners. Clip once if appearance of a true corner is desired.

Clip 3 or 4 times if corners are to be rounded.

535. Make SEAMS lay FLATTER around curves ... neck edges, facings, armholes, etc.

Press both seam allowances toward edge. TOPSTITCH on the facing 1/8" from seam.

Stitching will catch both seam allowances and facing. Facing will turn to the garment inside.

536. Interfaced SEAM ALLOWANCES look bulky. Trim interfacing so it is not caught in the seam allowance.

EXCEPTION: Sweater fabric and soft roll at center front fastening of a garment.

537. ALWAYS FINISH SEAM EDGES before sewing the garment.

538. Use SOFT NYLON NET as a seam binding. It leaves no bulk.

539. If the pattern instructs sewing a seam twice, ZIGZAG once instead.

540. Use hairline ZIGZAG stitches to sew Collars, Cuffs and Facings made from SHEERS.

Trim seam allowance as close as possible. Turn. Press well. Seam should be almost invisible.

541. Use a ZIGZAG or STRETCH STITCH to sew curves of underarm seams from notch to notch. Trim off excess seam allowance.

Sew in the same manner 6" to 7" of each seam from crotch toward top on BACK and FRONT of PANTS.

Seams have more strength and tolerate more stress in these areas.

542. Keep SHOULDER SEAMS FROM STRETCHING. Center polyester tape over seamline on WRONG side of the FRONT shoulder seam allowance.

Tape should be applied before seams are sewn.

543. FLAT SHOULDER SEAMS ON HEAVIER FABRIC ...

On RIGHT side of the fabric, PRESS both SEAM ALLOWANCES toward the back.

TOPSTITCH 1/4" from seam on the BACK catching both seam allowances.

Grade excess seam allowance on the INSIDE as close as possible to the stitching.

81

544. Sew several seams without cutting the thread.   After   all
     seams have been sewn, there's only ONE
     ACTION in clipping threads.

     Don't forget to backstitch at the
     beginning and end of each gar-
     ment piece.

545. SEAMS on WOOL/SILK
     COMBINATION FIBRES ...

     This type fabric will
     fray excessively. Be
     sure to have DEEP
     FINISHED SEAMS.

     DO NOT fit the garment
     too tight. There should
     be freedom of movement
     when garment is worn.

     Thread fibres will break   at   points where
     there is repeated strain due to flexing under tension.

546. Trim away FILLER in SEAM ALLOWANCES to avoid bulk in quilt
     fabric garments. Sews better too.

547. FLAT FELLED SEAMS should be used in
     QUILT fabric garments.

548. Trim seam allowances of garments made
     from SHEER fabrics to 1/4".

     It won't be necessary to clip or notch
     excess seam except for corners.

549. QUICK WAY to GRADE A SEAM
     ALLOWANCE ...

PRACTICE on SCRAPS
FIRST.

Place area to be graded between thumb
and hand, with index finger UNDER   seam
allowance.

Cut at an ANGLE so UPPER scissors blade is FLAT against
the fabric.

Index finger just under the scissors will feel direction
and keep garment from being cut.

Saves 3 to 5 minutes on each garment.

82

550. TOPSTITCH, <u>SEW STRAIGHT SEAMS</u> and STITCH–IN–THE–DITCH
like a professional ...

IT'S ALL IN THE PRESSER FOOT.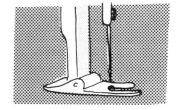

Rushed through a lovely new
dress only to find the topstitch looks like it was sewn after a
"night on the town" ...?? and

Your stitch–in–the–ditch looks like the "dam overflowed"
...?? and

Your **STRAIGHT SEAM** found its way 'round a curve that
wasn't even there ...??

Find the LITTLE GROVE in CENTER of the PRESSER
FOOT ... if presser foot doesn't have a "groove"
use the SIDE of the PRESSER FOOT as a GUIDE.

DO NOT LOOK AT THE NEEDLE AS YOU SEW. DO NOT LOOK
where you have been nor where you are.

<u>WATCH the "GROOVE" or "SIDE" of the PRESSER FOOT. It
will be easy to keep the needle moving in your direction
without leaving the sewing line.</u>

<u>NOTE</u>: The eye follows a moving object. If you're
watching the needle go up and down, it's impossible
to watch the seam direction.

551. TOPSTITCHES that are too small,
cause puckers.

Use <u>BASTING STITCHES</u> for TOPSTITCH-
ING.

552. ELIMINATE KNOTTED ENDS on HAND TOPSTITCHINNG THREADS
... At the beginning, leave 7" or 8" of thread hanging
free.

When project is finished, thread the needle
with hanging ends. Push into garment seam
allowance on the inside.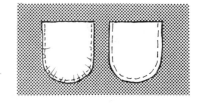

Tie off or fasten thread by sewing
several stitches in the seam
allowance.

Use the same methods to hide knots when sewing on buttons.

553. When using a contrasting thread to TOPSTITCH (as with Jeans), BOBBIN THREAD should MATCH the FABRIC. Jeans will be smashing and look nicer because each topstitch is definite.

554. Use BUTTONHOLE TWIST for TOPSTITCHING. It shows greater detail. (Also makes marvelous belt loops).

DO NOT USE BUTTONHOLE TWIST on SILK, SHEERS or FINE FABRICS.

555. A KITCHEN GLASS will "DO" ...

Topstitching with a DOUBLE NEEDLE gives the garment that "EXTRA TOUCH."

A second spool spindle is usually necessary to use a double needle.

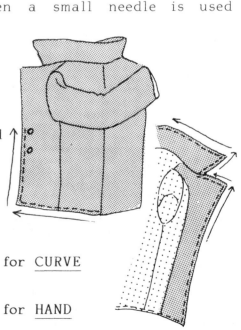

If your machine does not have an extra spindle, place the second thread spool in a glass. Place GLASS on RIGHT BACK SIDE of the machine. Thread the same as if there were two spool spindles.

556. Use a LARGE NEEDLE when DECORATIVE TOPSTITCHING with TWO THREADS.

There's too much friction when a small needle is used and threads break.

557. TOPSTITCH the JACKET so SPOOL THREAD is on the RIGHT SIDE of garment as it is being worn.

Start at CENTER BACK on the garment OUTSIDE. Stitch around front and up to the buttonhole/ button.

Turn jacket over. Continue topstitching on lapel to center back of the collar.

558. Use the machine QUILTING FOOT for CURVE TOPSTITCHING.

559. Use a VERY FINE SHARP NEEDLE for HAND TOPSTITCHING.

There's not much time saved by hand topstitching but

it can be very decorative, elegant, eyecatching and looks expensive.

DO IT RIGHT. Machine baste **NEXT** to the hand topstitching line. Make **EACH HAND STITCH** same LENGTH as the BASTING STITCH.

When finished, remove basting.

560. TOPSTITCHING FUR and PILE FABRICS ...

ALWAYS topstitch <u>with</u> the <u>GRAIN</u> of FUR/PILE fabrics.

Same is also true with **velvet, velour and corduroy.**

COLLARS, CUFFS and POCKETS

561. QUICKER CUFFS ... If pattern calls for TWO piece cuff, lay on the FOLD at seamline for a one piece cuff.

562. Use <u>PRE-MADE PURCHASED COLLARS</u> for Rugby and Polo Shirts. It saves at least 15 minutes sewing time.

There's a wide range of colors and a pre-made collar really makes the shirt look professional.

563. CUT the COLLAR and STAND as ONE ...

Overlap COLLAR and STAND patterns at SEAMLINES. Tape together and cut a new pattern.

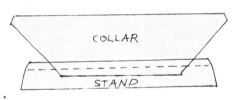

564. To keep it from rolling toward the front, TRIM off 1/8" from each side, of the UNDERCOLLAR, tapering to the point.

After sewing, front sides will roll slightly to underside.

565. For <u>NICER COLLAR POINTS,</u> be sure INTER-FACING is TRIMMED to stitching line and completely away from points.

566. <u>COLLAR POINTS LAY FLATTER</u> ... Stitch

collar to the point. PIVOT. Continue sewing. Trim seam allowance to 1/4" and POINTS to 1/8".

PRESS open seam allowances with a point presser.

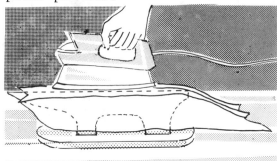

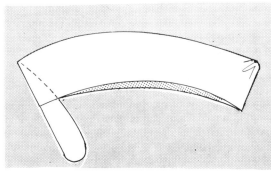

If a point presser is not available, lay collar flat on the ironing board. Press UPPER seam allowance toward collar.

Turn COLLAR, RIGHT sides out.

Use a POINT TURNER to push out collar points.

Press WRONG sides together, slightly rolling UPPER side to UNDER side.

Press stubborn areas with STEAM and CLAPPER part of the point presser.

567. Many times, UPPER and UNDER COLLAR pattern pieces are different sizes.

After cutting out, it's almost impossible to distinguish between UPPER and UNDER COLLAR.

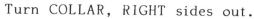

With marking pen, mark "P" on the UPPER collar and "N" on the UNDER collar after cutting out.

This will avoid sewing collars on backwards.

568. It's not uncommon for **purchased garments** to have "UNDER COLLAR HANG."

Make a TUCK along FOLD of the UNDER COLLAR, pulling excess to the UNDER side.

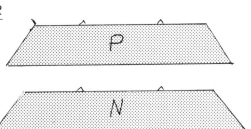

569. If COLLAR CORNERS look stretched out after stitching, begin at the corner. Sew away from the corner, NOT toward it.

570. ELIMINATE COLLAR UNDERHANG ... FOREVER.

Press open seam allowance of two collar pieces. Turn and press the collar, RIGHT SIDES out.

With UPPER COLLAR on TOP, gently work it toward the cut edges.

UPPER COLLAR will ROLL toward the UNDER COLLAR. UNDER collar will be a "smidge" longer than the UPPER COLLAR at cut edges.

Pin and baste in place. Trim off the longer UNDER COLLAR EDGE, even with the UPPER COLLAR.

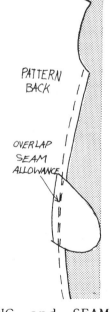

571. Make POCKETS PART of the GARMENT WITHOUT A SEAM. Overlap pocket and garment patterns, matching seams.

Cut the garment and pocket as ONE PIECE.

572. Keep the LINING of a PATCH POCKET from showing.

Cut the POCKET ONE INCH LONGER and the LINING ONE INCH SHORTER.

Fold the outside pocket on what would ordinarily be the pocket seamline.

573. Put an inch of INTERFACING across the top of any patch POCKET.

Top won't stretch.

574. KEEP THE POCKET CURVE ... Make the pocket pattern from cardboard. TRIM AWAY FACING and SEAM ALLOWANCE.

Cut pocket from fabric, using the regular pattern. DO NOT cut away seam allowance on fabric pocket.

Machine baste around curved edges. Place cardboard pattern on the pocket WRONG SIDE. Pull basting threads

87

until seam allowance curls around the cardboard edges.

Press.   Remove the cardboard pocket template.

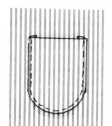

Position POCKET on the garment with GLUE STICK.   Sew.

Always use a L-O-N-G stitch to sew on pockets (5 or 6 stitches to the inch).

Turn pocket to the outside.   Remove basting stitches and trim seam allowance to 1/4".

575.   Use a <u>COMPATIBLE POCKET LINING</u> on JACKETS,   COATS, <u>MENS PANTS</u> ...

Pockets show through on light colored or lightweight fabric. This happens a lot on summer slacks for both men and women.

Make pockets from flesh tone or very light beige fabric. White pockets will show through white fabric.

Match darker fabric for darker colored garments.

576.   It's easy to have <u>EVEN POCKET PLACEMENT</u> on both sides of the garment.

Sew the FIRST POCKET in place.   Put SECOND POCKET, <u>FACE DOWN</u> on the first sewn pocket.

Position remaining garment FRONT section over the pocket and OPPOSITE SIDE.

Pin through fabric, catching the loose pocket.

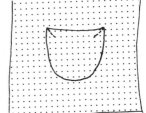

577.   <u>For PERFECT POCKET PLACEMENT</u>, mark stitching line on garment OUTSIDE.   Steam pocket in place with small strips of FUSIBLE WEB.

If satisfied with placement, **sew.**

578.   <u>POCKETS WILL NOT RIP</u> ...   Position pocket with Glue Stick.

<u>TOPSTITCH</u> (with basting stitch) on the pocket by starting 1/2" diagonally down from one corner.   Sew to the corner. <u>PIVOT.</u>   Continue down, around and to the opposite corner.   <u>PIVOT.</u>   Stitch downward, diagonally 1/2".

579. There are two pieces to many POCKETS. One pocket part is sewn to the garment **front** and one to the **back**. Then, both pocket pieces are joined.

BULK can be eliminated by pressing seam allowance of the pocket TOWARD THE POCKET, at FRONT and AWAY from the pocket on BACK.

(Seam allowance on BACK may need to be clipped).

580. For future POCKET SECURITY, sew a TRIANGLE on each side at the top.

$580\frac{1}{2}$. Not quick ... BUT CLASSY ..

Sew on PATCH POCKETS so all stitches are to the inside.

DO PRACTICE before trying the "real thing."

 THIS METHOD WORKS ONLY ON POCKETS WITH curves.

Press pocket seam allowance to the UNDER SIDE. Steam out excess fullness.

VERY IMPORTANT ... Mark the pocket position SEAMLINE on the garment with marking pen.

 Put heavy squares or dots on the seamline at various locations. Put two on the bottom, two on each side and one on each side at the curves.

Make corresponding marks at the same locations on the POCKET SEAM.

PINBASTE the POCKET in place on one side to the curve.

RIGHT SIDES TOGETHER, SEW. Be sure to match the MARKED positions of POCKET and garment.

It's easier than you think.

581. Like buttonholes, when slashing WELT POCKET OPENINGS, put a pin in all four corners.

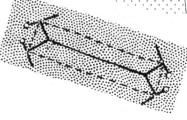

582. EASIEST and NICEST POCKET ... TRIM away FACING on the pocket PATTERN.

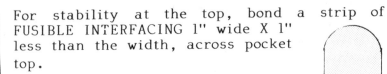

Fold the fabric HORIZONTALLY. Place top of pocket pattern on the fold. Cut.

Whole pocket may be INTERFACED ... OR ...

For stability at the top, bond a strip of FUSIBLE INTERFACING 1" wide X 1" less than the width, across pocket top.

Raw edge of the interfacing piece should be FLUSH with the pocket TOP at the fold.

Fold and pin RIGHT sides of the pocket together.

 Stitch. Trim seam allowance to 1/4".

Make a 2" slit in the center of the pocket UNDERSIDE.

(UNDERSIDE is the interfaced side).

Turn pocket RIGHT SIDES OUT through the slit and PRESS WELL.

Bond the slit together with small piece of fusible web on the pocket inside, just under the slit.

Position pocket on the garment with GLUE STICK and stitch. Press pocket with wet press cloth after stitching to garment

583. EASY WELT POCKETS ... Take it one step at a time.

Trace welt opening on TISSUE PAPER. Use scraps from tissue patterns. Pin to WRONG side of the fabric. Baste on welt opening lines.

Baste pocket and welts to RIGHT SIDE of the GARMENT. Prior basting stitch is used as a guide.

SEW AGAIN on the LONG WELT STITCHING lines, ON THE INSIDE. Backstitch at each end. SLASH the WELT.

Don't forget to PUT A PIN in each corner before slashing. TURN. TISSUE PAPER can be torn away and stitching never shows on the garment right side. Corners have been re-enforced.

584. Use TRANSPARENT TAPE to hold WELT POCKETS, BUTTONS, ZIPPERS, etc. in place until permanent stitching.

Remove all tape before applying heat.

Tape should not be the icky, sticky, gooey kind. Test on a scrap. It should peel off without effort or leaving residue. If it does not, look for another brand.

PRESSING/IRONING

585. Know the difference between PRESSING and IRONING ...

When PRESSING, the ironing is LIFTED and LOWERED. When IRONING, the iron is SLID back and forth over the garment.

586. Don't leave unfinished projects laying around. Place on a hanger until the next sewing session. You'll spend less time pressing.

587. Turn on the IRON/STEAMSTRESS one or two minutes before needed.

You can save a few seconds and be doing something else.

588. Garments will look better if PRESSED on an IRONING BOARD padded with WOOL. Imprints of areas like darts, seam edges, etc. will transfer to ironing board pad instead of garment.

Surely, there's an old WOOL army blanket in the surplus store.

589. Cover IRONING BOARD with STRIPED TICKING. Be sure the fabric will not fade.

Stripes can be used as a guide for folds, creases, pleats, etc.

590. Place an IRON HOLDER on the ironing board. Keeps iron out of the way when not in use. Also, reduces the risk of a small child being burned. Ask at the fabric shop.

591. STEAM IRON and STEAMSTRESS may be your TWO VERY BEST FRIENDS ...

NEVER press a garment with an iron directly on the fabric surface. Use a PRESS CLOTH between garment and iron.

My favorite is the STEAM-STRESS.

It exudes only steam. It will not scorch nor burn.

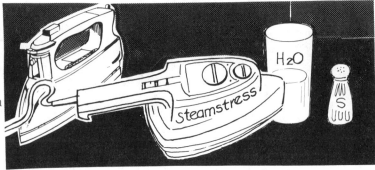

It will take out wrinkles, even when clothing or other items such as draperies, are in a hanging position.

The Steamstress operates on plain TABLE SALT and TAP WATER. Be sure to follow instructions for its use and cleaning.

592. Use an IRONING CORD GUIDE ...

Keeps the cord out of your way.

593. Ever wish you had a "toy" iron to get steam in all the small places of a sewing project?

KEEP A TRAVEL IRON in your sewing room. It will get steam to all the "tiny" places.

594. Usually, DISTILLED WATER is recommended for use in STEAM IRONS. If there is none, use regular tap water that has sat in a container for an hour or more. All minerals have gone to the bottom.

The next best thing is to use **WARM WATER** from the faucet. It comes out of the hot water heater. That water has been standing for a while with minerals settling to the bottom. Make sense?

595. Keep a small plastic bottle of WATER and baby food jar of TABLE SALT near the ironing board.

Makes an easy and quick "fillup" for the Steamstress.

596. Keep a SPRAY BOTTLE of WATER by the ironing board.

When a damp press cloth is needed, simply place cloth over the garment; spray and press.

597. Place a child's ironing board near the sewing machine for small pressing jobs. You won't have to get up.

598. 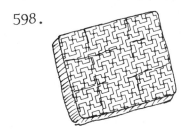 For SMALL PRESSING JOBS, pad and cover a KITCHEN CUTTING BOARD.

Leave on the sewing table.

599. PAD and COVER a ROLLING PIN. Also works well for pressing small areas.

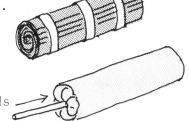

600. Cover the SLEEVE BOARD with a TUBE SOCK. It's great padding and saves a little money.

601. QUICK SLEEVE/SEAM ROLL from almost nothing ...

Roll magazines tightly. Tape to hold. Cover with pieces of old sheet.

Cut cover about 4 1/2" - 5" longer than the roll.

Use dowel or pencil to push cover ends into roll ends.

602. YARDSTICK, COTTON BATTING and a little ingenuity make a great PRESSING AID ...

Wrap a yardstick with cotton batting.

Place muslin or cotton fabric on the batting and pull together, tightly. Sew fabric together around the yardstick. After a little use, batting will round out.

Makes a terrific roll for pressing pant seams, sleeves and other hard-to-reach areas.

603. Press all STRAIGHT SEAMS open at the same time ...

604. Use of a PRESSING HAM helps rid the garment of puckers at shoulder edge and the "homemade" look... necessary for pressing curved seams.

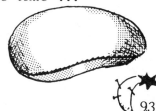

93

605. If more MOISTURE is needed for PRESSING and iron does not produce enough steam, place a piece of KITCHEN FOIL on the ironing board.

Press garment on top of the foil.

606. Wet two or three PRESS CLOTHS at one time.

Place in a Zip Loc bag. Attach to end of the ironing board with a clothespin ... OR ... put in the ironing board leg supports UNDERNEATH.

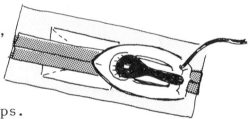

607. For PRESS CLOTHS, grandmother used an old DIAPER, clean DISH TOWELS and pieces from an old BEDSHEET.

One yard of white COTTON INTERLOCK will make two great PRESS CLOTHS. It holds steam heat, so necessary for "fusing" and two cloths will last about one year.

608. To prevent ridges on the gar- ment when PRESSING SEAMS open, place an envelope or sheet of paper folded in thirds, under seam allowance.

Using a POINT PRESSER also helps.

For PANTS, slip an empty FABRIC BOLT CARDBOARD CORE inside the leg to press seams open.

Press seams open on a SEAM ROLL.

If seams do not stay open after pressing, apply steam and press down with CLAPPER on bottom of the Point Presser.

Seam may also be pressed on the IRONING BOARD SIDE EDGE.

609. FOLD PATTERN INSTRUCTION SHEET and slip under seams when pressing.

They're handy and large enough for one iron length.

After use, it's quick and easy to refold and replace in the pattern envelope.

(One thing less to clean up after sewing).

610. FOLDED PAPER BAG STRIPS may be used under seams and

94

folds when pressing. WATCH FOR STAINS. Brown bags may stain when steam is applied.

611. DRAPERY BUCKRAM also prevents pressing marks.

    It's thin, doesn't stain, easily handled and can be rolled up when not in use.

612. BROWN PAPER BAG can be substituted for a PRESS CLOTH. Be sure it's clean and there's no grease, wax or other substance that comes off.

    Again ... beware of staining if moisture is applied.

613. If press cloth is not handy, wet TWO PAPER TOWELS. Squeeze out excess water. Place over areas to be pressed. Use once only.

614. Remind yourself not to fuse INTERFACING to the PRESS CLOTH.

    Mark little circles on the non-fusible side with a light blue, waterproof marking pen. No more "bloopers" with the interfacing.

615. For smoother PRESSING, run WARM IRON back and forth over a piece of WAX PAPER.

    Wipe excess wax from the bottom with a scrap. Iron will glide smoothly, almost without effort.

    (Learned that one from my grandmother when we used flat irons heated on the kitchen stove. It still works).

616. Prevent MILDEW when ironing is postponed. Add a little SALT to the sprinkling water.

    Wash any mildewed garment with a STRONG CONCENTRATION OF CHLORINE BLEACH.

617. Smaller parts of a garment such as POCKETS, BELTS, COLLARS and CUFFS should be pressed or ironed FIRST. Then, press or iron larger areas.

618. WRONG SIDE of CUFFS, YOKES, BELTS, COLLARS, etc. should be pressed or ironed first. Turn over and press the RIGHT SIDE. Outside will be flat and much neater.

619. To keep GATHERS from looking creased, press with iron tip.

620. DO NOT PRESS over pins or basting threads. Both leave marks. EXCEPTION: Silk Basting Thread generally does not leave marks if pressed.

621. DO NOT PRESS or IRON over buttons, belts, zippers or other garment decorations. It leaves a "ridge" and can damage fabric fibres.

622. DO NOT PRESS OR IRON UNCLEAN GARMENTS. Heat may seal in the soil.

623. DO NOT PRESS or IRON when you're upset or angry. Such emotions cause a "heavy hand" with the pressing aid.

Garments should be pressed or ironed with TLC.

624. For a SLIMMER LOOK, tucks and pleats should be pressed toward center of the garment.

625. CAREFUL WITH A HOT IRON on SYNTHETIC FABRICS ... If pressing instructions are lost and fabric content is not known, start by TIP PRESSING on the underside hem. if a scrap is not available.

Underside hem area can be repaired if scorched, burned or melted.

626. Before turning RIGHT SIDES out, all seams on COLLARS, CUFFS, FACINGS and other small pieces should be PRESSED OPEN.

TURN. Then piece should be pressed WRONG SIDES together. Point Presser makes the job a little easier.

627. Try on the garment BEFORE pressing in sharp creases such as pleats, zipper fly, pant creases.

628. PRESS with STRAIGHT GRAIN of the fabric. LIFT and PRESS.

Do NOT push the iron along. This is particularly important when applying fusible web or interfacing.

Do NOT "jiggle" or "wiggle" the iron. If you do, the fabric may "stretch" or "flare."

629. Using an EYEDROPPER, TINY SPONGE or BRUSH, put a small line of WHITE VINEGAR on crease lines.

Creases turn out real sharp after pressing.

Do TEST a scrap for discoloration before using vinegar on the garment.

630. For SHARP CREASES, wet PRESS CLOTH in solution ONE HALF WATER/ONE HALF WHITE VINEGAR.

Set iron on "WOOL." Press garment through the cloth until dry.

Test fabric scrap for vinegar effect on color before using.

631. PANT CREASES after COMPLETION ... Fold legs so side and inner leg seams are together.

Put pins in the seams to assure "togetherness." FOLD LINES SHOULD BE ON STRAIGHT of the FABRIC GRAIN.

Press from HEM to HIP on FRONT crease line with damp cloth and steam. Press from HEM to CROTCH LEVEL on BACK crease line.

Leave pants on the ironing board until completely dry.

632. If there are no pre-cutting alterations, PANTS may be creased before sewing. "Notch" crease line at TOP and BOTTOM of each pant leg.

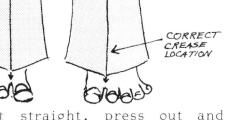

Fold from notch to notch.

Press in permanent crease on each leg. Sew the pants.

633. CORRECT LOCATION FOR PANT CREASE ... Press in light creases with steamstress.

Try on. STAND STRAIGHT and ERECT.

If creases point between BIG TOE and next SMALLER TOE, creases are straight and correct. If creases are not straight, press out and try again.

634. Instead of basting, PRESS in SMALL HEMS ...

635. PRESSING FABRIC with a NAP (Velvet, Corduroy, etc.) ... Place a scrap of the same fabric or loopy side of a fluffy

towel on the ironing board, RIGHT
SIDE UP. Lay garment RIGHT SIDE
DOWN on the scrap/towel and PRESS

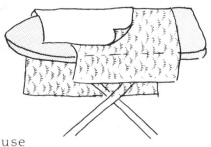

Scrap/towel loops and garment nap
will mesh. Seam allowances will
not "ridge" on the garment right
side.

DO NOT rest iron on the fabric ... use
STEAM only. Use a steamstress if possible.

636. PRESS LACE and EMBROIDERY on a folded WHITE TERRY
TOWEL.

Place RIGHT SIDE of lace/embroidery DOWN
on the terry. Press on WRONG side.

Designs will not look flat.

637. Use a NEEDLE BOARD to press VELVETS,
CORDUROYS and other high pile fabrics. Needle   Board   is
made   with   thousands   of   pins,   with   sharp   ends   mounted
upward, forming a flat surface.

638. Side seam POCKETS often refuse to lay flat.   They bulge
and gap, even when the garment fits loose.

Press POCKETS TO THE FRONT. Apply small
strip of fusible web to fuse front pocket
seam allowance to the garment.

Pocket will always stay in the correct
position.

639. For really sharp pleats, PRESS INSIDE and OUTSIDE ...
but do it by the rules.

Baste pleats in with SILK THREAD. Put
envelopes, paper bags or drapery buckram
under the fold.

Steam press on the garment INSIDE so crease
will not show on the outside. Allow pressed
area to cool.

Turn garment to outside. Remove basting
threads. Steam press pleat on OUTSIDE.

BEWARE: If basting threads are left in, thread
         marks will show on the outside.

640. Push different size <u>WOODEN DOWELS</u> inside ties, sashes, belts, etc. to PRESS open the seams.

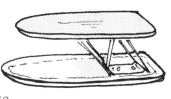

641. Always PRESS SEAMS in the DIRECTION in which they were sewn.

Use TIP of the iron, only. If you slide the iron, seam may be longer than other garment parts.

642. Use a <u>SLEEVE BOARD</u> to press open <u>SLEEVE SEAMS</u>.

Eliminates reverse creases in the sleeve.

643. Seams look better if presed to one side, before pressing open.

644. <u>ALWAYS press garment SEAMLINES after RIPPING.</u> Makes restitching much easier and helps restore fibres to their original position.

645. PRESS <u>SLEEVES</u> without leaving a crease ... Tightly stuff a <u>LARGE TUBE SOCK</u> with scraps. Close and sew the end. Place inside the sleeve and press with steam.

646. To avoid the "homemade" look <u>DO NOT PRESS SLEEVES FLAT.</u> Use a narrow sleeve board.

647. Press only <u>SEAM ALLOWANCE</u> of the <u>SET IN SLEEVE</u>.

This method is used by fine tailors.

It rids the sleeve of puckers particularly in the back.

648. Do <u>IRON LINEN</u> when it's DAMP.

DO NOT IRON LINEN PLEATS. They will crack and look old. PALM CREASE any pleats.

649. Iron <u>SILK</u> on a low setting, while damp. Watch out for steam. It may leave water marks on silk.

650. <u>DO NOT IRON SWEATERS.</u> If heat is needed, hold STEAM just above the area needing attention.

651. Use a HAIR BLOW DRYER and WET CLOTH to remove WRINKLES from clothing. Nice to know when travelling.

652. Move TAPEMEASURE out of the way when pressing.

Heat may melt the tapemeasure. Print could come off on the ironing board and you get "tapemeasure gooeys" on the garment.

653. PIN MARKS may be removed by pressing with cloth dampened in water/white vinegar solution.

Test a scrap for discoloration before using the vinegar.

654. After PRESSING, let the garment hang in an airy place for a few minutes.

It needs to cool and fibres should be completely dry before garment is placed in the closet.

655. On the road and forgot your travel iron? ...BUT NOBODY LEAVES HOME WITHOUT A CURLING IRON ...

Use it for an emergency, quick press-out.

Do test with the iron before trying to press. Would hate to see you at an IMPORTANT BREAKFAST MEETING with the shape of your curling iron burned in a sleeve.

Things about BUTTONS & BUTTONHOLES

656. Save EGG CARTONS for keeping BUTTONS.

Sort by color and put in the little "egg slots."

657. If garment hasn't been made or you don't want to take it "BUTTON SHOPPING" use a LARGE SCRAP.

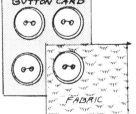

Make a slit in the scrap. Slip scrap onto the carded button to get an idea of its suitability for the garment.

658. LEAVE BUTTONS on the card until ready for use. (They're safer ... don't get lost).

Save small metal clips that hold shank buttons in place ... they come in handy later.

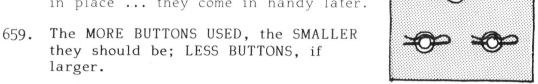

659. The MORE BUTTONS USED, the SMALLER they should be; LESS BUTTONS, if larger.

660. BUTTON on DRESS or BLOUSE NECKLINE should be placed same distance BELOW the NECKLINE as the measurement of ONE HALF the BUTTON'S DIAMETER.

661. BUTTONS from a PENNY ... To please a little boy, drill holes in a penny and sand for smoothness.

Five pennies will do for a little boy's shirt. Try to get five with the year of his birth.

If one is lost, it's easy and inexpensive to replace.

662. Easy BUTTON COVER ...

Sew BASTING STITCH AROUND the BUTTON COVER circle.

Place button in the center. Pull thread to gather in the fullness.

Apply under the button clamp.

663. BUTTON should be placed at the WAISTLINE only if there is no belt.

If THERE IS A BELT, button should be placed 1 1/2" above waistline.

664. Save scraps of pre-cut waist shaper.

Cut little pieces from the scraps to sew under BUTTONS for re-enforcement.

101

665. For better "staying power" seal center of <u>METAL BUTTONS</u> with clear nail polish.

666. Use BUTTON ELEVATOR to make a quick THREAD SHANK.

Follow package instructions.

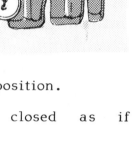

667. SEWING ON THE BUTTON ...

Tape button in place. Holes may be punched in the tape.

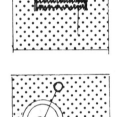

Also, GLUE STICK may be used for temporarily holding the button in position.

668. <u>BUTTON SEWING Kno-How</u> ... Pin garment closed as if it was buttoned.

Position straight pin at OUTER end of the buttonhole in the fabric <u>underneath</u>. Button center should be where the pin is located.

Make a stitch on RIGHT SIDE of the fabric at button position. Bring needle and thread through the button.

Place STRAIGHT PIN or small MATCH STICK across top of the button. Bring needle through the button and back down into the fabric.

Sew the button, going back and forth over the pin/match stick (toothpick will also work).

Remove pin/match/toothpick. Wrap thread around the threads UNDERNEATH the button. This forms a SHANK. Draw needle to the WRONG side and fasten thread. Cut.

669. Sew on FOUR HOLE BUTTONS, two holes at a time. Break thread between each sewing.

Buttons stay on longer.

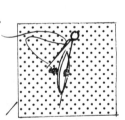

670. Use <u>EMBROIDERY FLOSS</u> to sew on BUTTONS ... Pull thread through button-holes <u>ONCE</u> and tie off.

SEW TWO HOLES — TIE OFF — SEW OTHER TWO HOLES

671. Use <u>NYLON FISHING LINE</u>, DENTAL FLOSS, BUTTONHOLE TWIST, or <u>HEAVY DUTY CARPET</u> thread to sew on the heavier shank-type buttons. (Use dental floss for light colors).

672. Take less strokes in and out of BUTTON EYES. Thread needle with FOUR STRANDS instead of two.

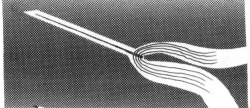

673. Another way to SECURE the BUTTON ...

Put CLEAR NAIL POLISH on the thread after button is sewn on. Thread won't come out or unravel.

674. BUTTON RE-ENFORCEMENT ... For durability, place a small fabric square or smaller button on REVERSE side of garment under the button.

675. Instead of sewing on SHANK BUTTONS with thread, place STRAIGHT "EYE" of a hook & eye, through the shank. Sew on the "STRAIGHT EYE."

It should hold on the shank button for life of the garment.

676. Sew on BUTTONS at the NECK of MENS SHIRT with ELASTIC THREAD. Button will "give" a little and be more comfortable.

677. If finger or hand handicap causes problems with cuff buttons, SEW BUTTONS ON with ELASTIC THREAD ... easier to manage ... OR

... Instead of buttonhole, place a VELCRO CIRCLE under the button.

Buttons may be eliminated altogether if elastic is used at sleeve edge. Also, sleeve cuff may be cut on the bias, just long enough to slip over the hand. Bias cut will stretch a little and buttons aren't necessary.

678. On DRESSES and BLOUSES, BUTTONS should be sewn on, so there is 1/4" from BUTTON EDGE to FOLD of the facing.

There should be 3/8" for JACKETS and 1/2" for COATS.

Generally, buttons are sewn on center front line. Choose button size accordingly.

679. Hammer-on SNAP FASTENERS, machine applied SELF GRIPPING

or other type fasteners may be used instead of buttons.

680. ALWAYS have a BUTTON or FASTENER between BUST HIGH POINTS. Eliminates gapping.

681. Choose BUTTONS after garment is made. What looks good on flat fabric may be "awful" after garment completion. It's wise to take the garment along for button selection.

682. For a really FEMININE LOOK, trim buttons with RIBBONS.

Put the ribbon through buttonholes and tie. Sew buttons in place.

683. A better COVERED BUTTON ... Dampen button fabric cover piece.

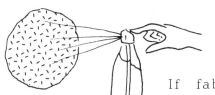

Better to spray with water, than douse and squeeze.

If fabric is likely to shrink, cut the cover piece a "smidge" larger than usual.

Apply button cover while damp and let dry. It's easier and results in a snugger fit on the button.

If button metal is likely to rust because of the damp cover, apply coat of nail polish before covering. Do let the polish dry before cover application.

684. Apply lightweight, FUSIBLE INTERFACING to FINE, SLIPPERY or SHEER button cover fabric.

Interfacing sheer fabric will also eliminate button metal shine.

Easier if fabric is interfaced before cutting out button cover circles.

685. REMOVABLE BUTTONS for CLEANING ... Put an EYELET in the fabric at button position.

Place button shank through the EYELET to inside. Hold button in place with SMALL METAL CLIPS from carded shank buttons (remember I told you to save these in Tip No. 658).

For NON-SHANK type buttons, make a BUTTONHOLE on EACH SIDE of the garment in corresponding locations.

104

Cut a piece of GROSGRAIN RIBBON, same size as the button-hole. Sew a button on each side of the ribbon.

← BUTTON
GROSGRAIN
← BUTTON

Be sure THREAD SHANK is long enough to go through fabric thickness. When garment is closed, one button is INSIDE and one is OUTSIDE.

Do have a specific place for BUTTON SAFEKEEPING when garment is cleaned.

686. Put FLAT BUTTONS between two strips of Magic Transparent Tape about 1/8" apart.

Cut and peel off tape as buttons are needed. These can be pinned to or hung on the board above the sewing machine for quick visibility and easy reach.

687. SAVE EXTRA BUTTONS ...

Sew to a scrap of the garment fabric.

Put in the button box. Scrap makes it easy to find if a garment button is lost.

688. If buttons outlive the garment, re-move with a seam ripper.

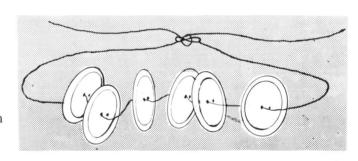

Thread onto a DOUBLE STRAND of DENTAL FLOSS with large darning needle.

Tie floss ends together and put in the BUTTON BOX. Color and number are easy to see.

689. Cover all your neat, BREAKABLE BUTTONS with ALUMINUM FOIL before washing the garment.

690. Learn to make BOUND BUTTONHOLES. They are used by designers for an EXPENSIVE look.

Get a book; take a class; practice until YOUR buttonhole looks professional.

691. Make the CORRECT SIZE BUTTONHOLE ...

Wrap tapemeasure around the entire button. Divide measurement by two, which is the CORRECT BUTTONHOLE SIZE. Make buttonhole size accordingly.

692. Another method to get CORRECT SIZE BUTTONHOLES is to measure button's DIAMETER; add HEIGHT of the button AND 1/8".

693. If making more than one garment, using the same color thread, make ALL BUTTONHOLES at one time.

694. If working with STRIPES, put all buttonholes on ONE STRIPE.

It's real classy to use buttons that match the stripe on which buttons are sewn.

695. EASY-TO-SEE BUTTONHOLE MARKING ...

Put a small piece of masking tape

alongside line to be used for the buttonhole. Keeps you on the "straight and narrow."

MASKING TAPE

Also, buttonhole may be marked with a very THIN LINE of NAIL POLISH.

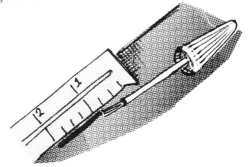

Cuts out when buttonhole is slit.

If WATER ERASABLE marking PENS or PENCILS are used to mark buttonhole locations, REMOVE MARKINGS before slashing the buttonhole.

696. BUTTONHOLE TEMPLATES are available in various sizes. They're easy to use and do save time. Ask at your fabric shop.

697. There will be NO FRAYING if NYLON SHEER TRICOT is cut on the grain for facing bound buttonhole areas.

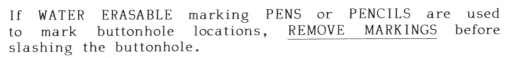

698. Put TISSUE PAPER or adding machine tape under SHEER FABRIC when making the button-holes.

Tear away paper after buttonholes have been completed.

699. Stabilize BUTTONHOLES on LOOPY, SWEATER and other LOOSE WEAVE fabrics, without interfacing.

Place a small piece of FUSIBLE WEB over the buttonhole area. Mark buttonhole on the fusible web.

Sew the buttonhole. Pull out fusible web.

Sew the buttonhole with a LOOSE ZIGZAG stitch (NOT WITH a buttonhole attachment apparatus).

Do NOT apply heat of any kind until all fusible web has been removed.

700. INVISIBLE BUTTONHOLES ... FLY FRONT for HEAVY FABRIC garments ... BUTTONHOLES DON'T SHOW.

Make VERTICAL BUTTONHOLES on 1" or more width GROSGRAIN RIBBON (instead of through all garment thicknesses).

Ribbon should be at least 1 3/4" longer at the TOP and BOTTOM, than is needed for buttonhole area.

Sew BUTTONHOLED RIBBON to facing BEFORE facing is stitched to garment front.

Sew ribbon to facing on back edges, TOP and BOTTOM. Ribbon should lay flat on the facing.

You may stitch between buttonholes; but leave enough room so garment can be buttoned with ease.

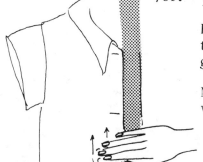

701. BUTTONHOLES in KNIT fabrics ...

Knits will stretch during attempt to make buttonholes on the cross grain ... but it can be fixed.

Mark proper buttonhole length with a marking pen.

Place fingers on each side of the buttonhole while sewing and STRETCH the FABRIC VERTICALLY as much as possible.

Buttonhole should come out the correct size.

702.	Another good way to make BUTTONHOLES on STRETCH or KNIT fabric ...

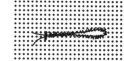

Stitch buttonhole over PERLE COTTON CORDING. Make a loop with the cording.

Looped end should be toward the garment opening. There is more stress in this part of the buttonhole when garment is fastened.

When buttonhole is finished, gently pull cording ends AWAY from the garment opening. This eliminates any stretch that may have occurred during stitching.

When it is apparent buttonhole is the correct size, thread each CORD END into a tapestry needle and pull to the UNDERSIDE. Tie off and clip the excess.

703.	Use VERTICAL BUTTONHOLES on garments with FRONT DECORATIVE BANDS.

VERTICAL buttonholes do add a 'touch of class.'

704.	VERTICAL buttonholes are blamed for "gap-osis" and front "pop-open."

The problem can be completely ELIMINATED.

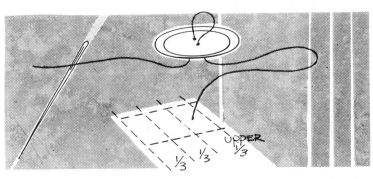

Divide buttonhole into THIRDS.

Lap buttonhole OVER the BUTTON SIDE.

Sew on button so it will be in UPPER ONE THIRD of the buttonhole.

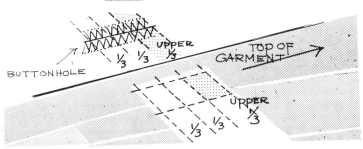

Be sure buttonhole is the correct size for chosen button.

(See Tip Nos. 691 and 692 on correct buttonhole sizing).

705. HORIZONTAL buttonholes are okay on FOLD-BACK FACINGS.

706. VERTICAL buttonholes should be on the CENTER FRONT line.

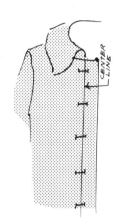

HORIZONTAL buttonholes start a "smidge" BEYOND center line, toward the front.

If HORIZONTAL buttonhole is started exactly on the center front line, button will be too far to the left.

707. Keep BOTTOM button on the blouse from showing under skirt or pants.

Make buttonhole on the left side. Sew button on the UNDER, RIGHT SIDE.

Sew on a FLAT BUTTON. It doesn't have to match the others.

708. Garment may be uncomfortable if a belt wraps over a button at the waist.

Make a buttonhole on LEFT side of the garment. Sew button to the UNDER, RIGHT side of the garment.

When garment is closed, button will be on the inside and "belt lump" is gone.

709. For TIES in WRAP SKIRTS, SLANT the BUTTONHOLES. They will stand more wear and tear.

710. Buttonholes may be slashed with a seam ripper. Do it in the DAYLIGHT. It's much easier to see.

711. AVOID TRAGEDY ... Place a pin at each end of the buttonhole before slashing.

712. The very best tool I have found to cut open buttonholes accurately and safely is the BUTTONHOLE CUTTER. Ask at the fabric shop.

713. Put FRAY STOP or FRAY CHECK on buttonholes and back of each button. Buttonhole threads won't ravel and buttons won't fall off.

714. If LIGHT COLOR INTERFACING has been used with dark fabric, threads will show when buttonhole is cut. COLOR fraying INTERFACING thread with a DARK FELT PEN.

715. Hide a "grungie" VERTICAL buttonhole and make garment front look great, at the same time.

Place a small button at each end of the vertical buttonhole.

It's unusual, pretty, functional and can hide a "blooper."

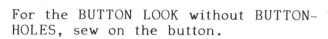

716. For the BUTTON LOOK without BUTTON-HOLES, sew on the button.

Place VELCRO on the underside.

Velcro comes in various colors; keep a little of each on hand.

717. Use an EXPANDABLE SEWING GAUGE for fast, accurate spacing of buttons/buttonholes, hooks & eyes, dress and drapery pleats, tucks, shirring and smocking.

It's also a good knitting gauge and handy for most quilting measurements.

718. Sew BUTTONS, HOOKS & EYES and other fasteners, on with sewing machine. It's faster. Your machine manual should have instructions.

719. Sew fasteners onto waistband before finishing. Belt will cover stitches.

HEMS and HEMMING

720. Kids use your HEM MARKER for a "sub machine gun?" ...

Borrow the BATHROOM PLUNGER. Place a rubber band at the appropriate hem length.

721. Place a METAL SEAM GUIDE inside the HEM ALLOWANCE. Press as depth of the hem is being measured. Seam guide eliminates press mark of the fabric cut edge.

722. HEMMING SHEERS and FINE fabrics with FUSIBLE WEB or GLUE.

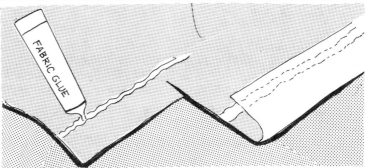

Press up hem with steam. If fusible web is used, place small 1/2" wide strips between garment and hem.

Seal 3" to 5" at a time with steam only. After all adjustments, HEM may be permanently pressed with damp press cloth.

Do NOT use GLUE or FUSIBLE WEB without TESTING. Even if fusible web can be used, do NOT baste it to the hemline without testing. Basting thread may show through to RIGHT side.

723. LETTUCE EDGE ... QUICK HEM on KNITS ... Fold up 1/4" to 3/8".

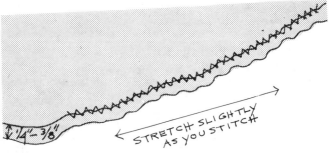

Stretch lightly.

Zigzag on the fold as it is being stretched.

WARNING: Test a scrap.

Lettuce edge hem is NOT SUITABLE for WOVENS and INTER-LOCKING STITCH fabrics.

724. If marks remain after lengthening a garment, CAMOUFLAGE it.

Turn it into a WELT STITCHED edge. To make the welt, stitch along mark and then again 1/4" below it.

To see if you like the look, draw a line on the garment with chalk. Works very well on wools.

725. When using bulky fabrics, dispose of a thick look in the hem at seams.

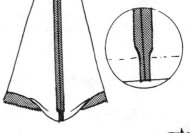

After hem is pressed in place, cut off HALF the seam allowance from lower edge to 1/8" ABOVE the HEM FOLD LINE. This method also works well on sleeve hems.

111

726. Another way to rid the bulky hem of a thick look is to
CUT A NOTCH in SEAM ALLOWANCES on EACH
side of the seam at HEMLINE.

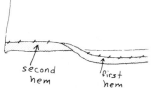

727. Small LEAD WEIGHTS inside a hem may
help the garment hang more evenly.

728. Narrow hems on knits will sometimes flip
up to the garment right side.

Cut the garment 1/2" to 3/4" longer.   Turn up a small
hem and stitch in place.

Turn up the hem a second time and stitch.

First stitching will also keep fabric from
rolling inside the hem.

On children's clothes, second hemming
may be let out as the child grows.

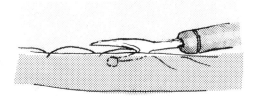

729. NEED TO LENGTHEN a READY-TO-WEAR garment?   Clip thread
between two loops on chain
stitched hems.   Pull one end ...
ravels out.

Use small scissors or nippers for
clipping.

Use SEAM RIPPER to rip out hand
sewn hem.

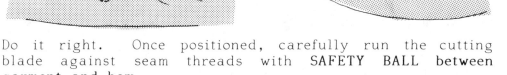

Do it right.   Once positioned, carefully run the cutting
blade against seam threads with SAFETY BALL between
garment and hem.

If the hem hung straight, old crease line may be used
as a guide to shorten or lengthen.

If the old crease does not come out with pressing, try
a little white vinegar on it.   Press.   WARNING: Test
fabric scrap for discoloration before using vinegar.

If vinegar doesn't work, cover the crease with TRIM,
RUFFLE, LACE or DECORATIVE STITCH.   Add a little of
the same on garment to make it look "intended."

730. To rid a dress of static cling, place small safety pins inside the hem.

731. HEM the FORMAL within 1/2" of the floor in BACK. BEWARE "floor touching" in the front or you'll be on your nose instead of your toes. DRESS SHOULD TOUCH SHOE TOPS AT TOES in FRONT.

732. Nice way to HEM VERY SHEER/FINE fabrics ...

Measure 1/2" from the edge to be hemmed. Stitch on the 1/2" mark

Press up 9/16" to UNDERSIDE.

With hem in place, sew between the hem fold and first row of stitching.

Cut off first 1/2" of hem as close as possible to the first row of stitching. (Works on bias cuts too).

733. Use a little HORSEHAIR BRAID in hems of garments made with SILK, QIANA and other lightweight fabrics.

After it has been marked and pressed, place braid inside the HEM with EDGE TOUCHING the CREASE. Ease it to the garment so width is not distorted. (Braid stretches like bias).

You may want to add a second or third strip of braid if one is not enough.

734. If you have MORE in the BACK than front, HEM DRESSES and SKIRTS LONGER in back. Garment hangs and feels better.

735. Before hemming JACKET, try it on with pants or skirt with which it is to be worn.

Hem to the length most flattering to your figure. Jacket will look nicer if it's 1/2" longer in back than front.

736. HAND SEW HEMS with a LIGHT TOUCH. Stitches should be loose or garment right side will have "pox" marks in area of the hem.

737. EASY HAND HEMMING ... Place pins on
RIGHT side of the garment after hem has
been pressed in place.

Threads won't catch on the pins. Saves
time.

738. HAND ROLLED HEMS are best for bias
cuts in lightweight fabrics.

739. After washing, many BIAS cut
skirts hang lower on one side
than the other.

Tape skirt band to the refrigerator door.
Make sure it's HORIZONTALLY STRAIGHT.

Let it hang overnight. Re-hem.

740. HEM in a CIRCULAR or BIAS CUT SKIRT
should never be more than 1" ...
1/2" is even better.

Turn up 1/2" and press. Use a fine
SATIN STITCH on the hem edge. Cut
away excess fabric from WRONG side.

741. EASY WAY TO HEM a CIRCULAR SKIRT ... Make two rows
of basting stitches 1/4" apart and 1/4" from skirt edge.

Turn up hem and pull bobbin threads to
ease in fullness. After hemming,
remove basting.

742. SHORTEN the FLARED
or CIRCULAR SKIRT
without frustration.

Measure up desired
distance from lower
edge. Mark 2" or 3" from the side seam.

Starting at the side seam, cut away excess
along markings.

Fold in the bottom edge and use as a
guide to cut 2" or 3". Follow pro-
cedure to the center.

Repeat on opposite side.

743. HEM will never be LOPSIDED ... Pin waistband of circular

114

skirt across straight line of a hanger. Let hang for 7 or 8 days before hemming.

If fabric is washable, dip skirt in water. Hang up wet (don't wring). Let it drip dry and hem.

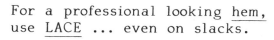

744. For a professional looking hem, use LACE ... even on slacks.

Woven fabric won't ravel and there's less lumping on the hemline.

745. Use FUSIBLE WEB for HEMMING. When fusing hems in knit garments, one turn-up is sufficient.

Hems in WOVENS may be fused also. One turn-up is enough IF fusible web is FLUSH with the raw edge.

Fusible web stabilizes the fibre. If fraying persists, use FRAY STOP or FRAY CHECK.

746. When HEMMING, to keep Fusible Web from slipping, baste it to WRONG side LOWER edge of the garment.

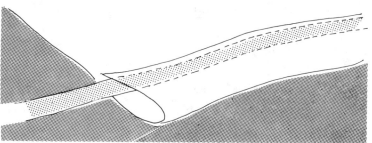

Using a gauge, turn up the hem and PIN in place, 5" to 6" apart.

Seal in hem and STEAM between pins, just enough to hold until permanent pressing.

Do NOT PRESS over PINS. Marks may not press out.

Remove pins. Press in permanent hem. Use damp press cloth and iron on wool setting.

747. If Fusible Web is used in PANT LEG, seal HEMS PERMANENTLY before pressing in CREASES.

If hems are not permanently sealed, a small double pleat may appear on the inside at crease points.

748. Try WASHABLE FABRIC GLUES for hemming. Ask at the fabric shop. Follow package instructions and DO TEST "glue" on a scrap before using.

749. HEM and SEW DECORATION on at the same time ... Turn hem UP, RIGHT sides together.

Place decorative lace or trim on UPPER side, covering turned up hem. Stitching shows on TRIM and hems at the same time.

750. Use small amount of SPRAY STARCH on CHIFFON, QIANA and other soft slippery fabrics to help ROLL NARROW or CIRCULAR, ruffle-type edges.

751. Dampen fingers with water when sewing a hand-rolled hem. Easier to handle sheer and fine fabrics.

752. Easy ROLLED HEM on THIN, SHEER or FINE fabrics ...

Give it body by stitching very close to the edge. Cut away excess to the stitching.

Roll between thumb and finger. Use tiny slipstitches at top of the fold.

753. The 1/4" finished ROLLED HEM on SHEERS and FINE fabrics

... Turn up 1/2". Pickstitch horizontally 1/4" from the cut edge, all around.

... Turn FOLD up 1/4" (fold should just cover raw edge).

... Slipstitch fold to the garment.

754. If destitute and have no Pins, Basting Tape or Glue Stick, use CLOTHESPINS to hold HEM in place.

(Do not leave clothespins on hem indefinitely: may cause indentations in the fabric.

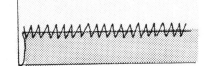

755. Turn up HEM with GLUE STICK. Adjustments are quick. There are no pin marks.

Sewing is quicker because there are no pins to remove.

756. HEM GAUGE is a real TIME SAVER. The investment is small and rewards are great. Hem may be turned up in half the time.

757. ZIGZAG a QUICK HEM. Turn under once. Catch raw edges in the zig-zag stitch. Decorative too.

758. MAKING a SURVIVOR ... Everyone should know how to hem.

Once I saw a lovely airline stewardess with a STAPLED hem. She had never learned that simple skill. (Aren't you sorry for such a soul)?

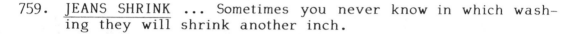

Then ... there's the hem that's pinned or glued by Elmer. Really sad.

One lady suggested that she made her daughter a "survivor" by pulling the hem out of each dress or skirt before hanging in the youngster's closet.

Youngster did learn to "hem."

759. JEANS SHRINK ... Sometimes you never know in which washing they will shrink another inch.

Before washing, fold up the hem and secure in place with MASKING TAPE. Tape will not come off in the wash.

Try on. If Jeans are too short, lower hem and replace masking tape.

Do this for 3 or 4 washings until shrinkage has stopped. Then permanently hem to desired length.

THIS 'n THAT KNOWLEDGE 'BITS'

760. All BEGINNERS should practice sewing with TWO LAYERS of fabric. Majority of sewing is with double layers. Beginner should get used to it.

761. SAVE TIME SHOPPING ... Shop during the dinner hour. Everyone else is home and the store may be exclusively yours.

762. The SEWING ORGANIZER is really handy. It holds thread, bobbins, scissors, pins and just everything.

Sides fold out when in use. Sides fold "up" and lock when not in use. Ask at the fabric shop.

763. DIVERT ATTENTION ... Choose a small print to make the garment requiring special skills.

If you "blow it" print diverts attention from your "goof."

764. BUY QUALITY ... Do NOT buy

  ...   Something just because it's "inexpensive" or "cheap."
  ...   Elastic that has no memory or rolls.
  ...   Fusible Web that washes out.
  ...   Thread that shrinks, fades, rots or knots up in the machine.

765. Do NOT buy fabric from a THUMBNAIL SWATCH ... At least a 6" square is needed to see small print. Square should be larger if print is big.

Selecting SOLID COLORS is an EXCEPTION.

766. SET GOALS for YOURSELF ... Set a time to CUT ... a time to PRESS ... a SPECIFIC DATE on which the garment is to be completed.

Write it all down and pin on the sewing board. Check off each accomplishment with a colored pen or pencil. If you're ahead of schedule, give yourself a gold star or small treat.

767. "GRUNGIE CUTICLES" snag knits and fine fabrics. Soak YOUR FINGERS in WHITE VINEGAR every day for one week, and then, once every 3 or 4 days. Snagging cuticles will disappear.

If hands have cuts and cracks, a good "VINEGAR SOAKING" will also act as a "healing" agent.

768. SCRATCHY and ROUGH HANDS will improve if rubbed with a TEAPOON of SALAD OIL and SUGAR. Wash thoroughly with soap and rinse well.

Use favorite hand cream.

769. CAREER WOMAN ...

Take your handwork on business trips. Do it on a plane or in the hotel, watching television. Plan your wardrobe to wear, if the garment is finished while traveling.

770. Add PIN TUCKS to the bodice-back of a dress or basic blouse pattern before cutting the fabric.

Pin tucks make broad shoulders look more narrow and the shorter figure, look taller.

771. Sew TUCKS on the garment OUTSIDE for decoration.

772. Ladies who are SHORT or carry EXTRA WEIGHT should NOT wear pants with cuffs. Cuffs give the illusion of SHORTER and WIDER.

773. DARK COLORS can make "large lumps" look SMALLER ... not that any of us have such things.

774. DULL FINISH FABRICS give the illusion of "SMALL."

775. Short SIDE SLITS on SHORTS make thighs look SMALLER and LEGS look LONGER.

776. Wearing a blouse "outside" doesn't make you look thinner ... just sloppy.

777. KEEP PANT LEGS inside BOOTS ... Make elastic stirrups. Sew one end of elastic to each side of the pant leg at lower edge.

Use just enough elastic to go around bottom of the foot and don't pull too tight.

778. To hold shirttail in place, try tucking inside your pantyhose.

Gets rid of the shirttail line under skirts and pants too.

779. UNDERWEAR made from natural fibres, especially SILK will retain body heat. You stay warm from the inside.

It's lightweight and can be worn with comfort under nice clothes. (Really expensive in ready-to-wear; aren't you glad you can sew).

780. Thermostat can be lowered 3 1/2 degrees by merely wearing a medium weight sweater.

781. Do wear a HAT on COLD DAYS.   One fourth of the body's

heat goes to the head. Major portion of body heat will be lost if the head is not covered.

782. <u>NYLONS will not CLING if rubbed with HAND LOTION.</u>

783. If funds are limited for dressing up the wardrobe, make a WINTER WHITE JACKET, PANTS or SKIRT.

   This color can always be worn with other colors.

784. Wear <u>WOOLENS ONLY ONE DAY at a time.</u>

   Fibres stretch and garment bags if worn two days in a row.

   After each wear, brush lightly with a soft fingernail brush and let it rest.

   Peeling on wool garments can be shaved off with a razor. Be careful not to shave too close.

785. Make sure the <u>COLOR WHITE being worn is NO WHITER than your TEETH.</u>

   If color is whiter, TEETH will look DARKER.

786. Wear <u>NUDE or FLESHTONE UNDERGARMENTS under SHEER</u> fabrics. "Nude" under black is better than "black" under black. If any other color is worn, "undies" will "tattle."

787. When wearing two colors that do not match, add a bright contrasting color for distraction.

   If brown jacket and brown skirt are made from TWO different dye lots, wear a bright yellow blouse. Add a yellow/brown print scarf to tie in all garment colors.

788. Wear a <u>COTTON SLIP under BIAS CUT GARMENTS.</u> It will help to hold garment shape.

789. Do be careful which CLEANER is used. They don't seem to know much about pressing bias cut garments WITH THE GRAIN.

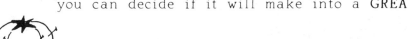

790. If you're not sure the new dress pattern will fit or look right on you, make it up in a NIGHTGOWN. If it looks and fits okay as a nightgown, you can decide if it will make into a GREAT DRESS.

791. PANTS BAGGY in the rear and just below the seat on legs?

Try pinching a 3/8" fold in center back pant legs pattern from waist to foot on the crease.

Crease line will be changed; so watch for this when pressing in permanent creases.

If "pinch" causes tightness in the waist area, cut pant sides a little straighter. This will compensate for fabric taken out of the back.

792. Use old sheets to avoid "DUST COLLECTION" on your nice things.

Drycleaner bags seem to be a favorite "recycle" for storing clothes out of season.

BEWARE ... EVIL LURKS IN THOSE BAGS. Most are made from Polyvinyl chloride. As the bag ages, it deteriorates into hydrochloric acid. White garments may get BROWN spots if covered too long with such a bag.

793. If clothing is left hanging in the closet over a long time, SLEEVES GET FLAT. STUFF SLEEVES WITH TISSUE PAPER when stored for the season.

794. OLD SHIRT - NEW LOOK ... Cut cuffs off sleeves. Trim enough off lower cut edges to make EPAULETS (or tubing).

Sew a narrow hem on each sleeve. Sew Epaulet end INSIDE at SLEEVE CENTER, 6" to 7" from the shoulder.

Roll up the sleeve. Pull Epaulet down and UP, over sleeve roll, toward the shoulder. Button or sew in place.

If the Epaulet is wide, a vertical buttonhole may look pretty "spiffy" here.

795. Eliminate the "CLINGING" skirt or dress. Wear Tricot slip TURNED INSIDE OUT, underneath.

796. If you get 'itches' from WOOL GARMENTS, wear a BODYSUIT underneath.

797. TERRY CLOTH makes great PAJAMAS for everyone from 1 to 98.

Cotton terry is cool in summer and warm in winter. They

are practically indestructible. I've slept in a pair for five years ... replaced elastic and ribbed cuffs three times. They're good for at least three more years.

798. If you have trouble matching colors, charts are available at most fabric shops. **Ask.** Some shops teach classes in garment coordination.

799. EASY MENDING ... Place thin tissue paper under the area to be mended.

Sew back and forth.

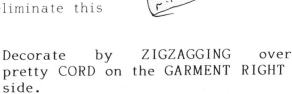

THIN PAPER UNDER FABRIC

800. After much laundering, LINT BALLS may accumulate in pockets, dart ends, cuffs and hems.

Without ripping out these areas, pick the lint out with a small CROCHET HOOK.

Push gently between stitches and hook the lint balls.

(Using fusible web may eliminate this problem in hems).

801.

Decorate by ZIGZAGGING over pretty CORD on the GARMENT RIGHT side.

802. QUICK MEND .. Press damaged area. Fuse interfacing to the WRONG side.

803. Use TRANSPARENT NYLON Thread for machine mending. It blends with all colors and thread doesn't have to be changed with each garment.

804. To mend hole or tear in KNIT or SWEATER fabric, place GAUZE BANDAGE under the area. Sew back and forth.

805. PANTYHOSE lasts LONGER ... Handwash. Rinse well. Soak 2 or 3 minutes in any "rinse-off" type hair conditioner.

806. QUICK BELT ... Fuse fabric to pre-stiffened commercial belting.

Sew VELCRO to UNDERSIDE of the TOP OVERLAPPING end. Sew mate VELCRO on TOP of the UNDER BELT END in the appropriate location for your waist size. PLAIN but ELEGANT.

Use a DECORATIVE PIN to "spiff" up the belt. Remove for use on other garments, washing and cleaning. VERY VERSATILE.

807. WAISTLINE not PROPORTIONATE to the HIP MEASUREMENT? Hard to pull on pants? ...

Pull pants up to the knees. CROSS one foot over the other. Flinch buttock muscles and "wiggle" in slowly.

This little exercise will also reduce hip measurement if the "flinch" is held two minutes, five or six times daily.

808. Pants will come out of the wash with SAME CREASE LINES if legs are pinned together at lower edge.

809. Mend the HOLE-LY SWEATER with a square of NYLON on the UNDERSIDE. Gives the area stability and mending time is cut in half.

810. Next time you make a JACKET, reverse the OVERLAPPING VENT. Put it on the RIGHT instead of left side.

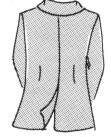 

When entering an automobile, the left vent will not be pushed up and pressed into a crease with body heat.

811. Put the BACK, OPEN SIDE VENT of a WRAP SKIRT on the LEFT.

It will not open when sliding onto the car seat.

812. YOKES are lovable ... but only for those who can wear them.

Make yokes HIGH if you're BIG-BUSTED. "Little busts" can wear yokes anywhere, any time.

Don't wear garments with BACK YOKES if you have ROUND or BROAD SHOULDERS.

813. Do NOT throw away the EXTRA piece of YARN that comes with a SWEATER. Thread a tapestry needle and weave the yarn into one of the sweater seams. You may have

to use it for mending later and thread will get the same wash and wear as garment.

Yarn will not be darker or lighter than the garment when used and it won't get lost in a deep, dark sewing drawer.

814. RAVELING KNITTED BAND ... If thread unravels in both directions, roll band and hold as a fist.

Pull thread.

Band does not dangle and raveling is twice as quick.

815. Repair SNAGS in KNITS and SWEATERS with NEEDLE THREADER ... Push the threader through fabric from the WRONG side.

Catch the snag and pull it through from RIGHT to WRONG side.

816. SNAGS may be fixed with a TOOTHPICK also ...

If there is no KNIT PICKER, SNAG FIXER or other snag repair tool, surely you have a toothpick.

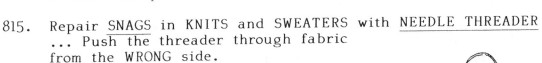

Use LARGE END to push the "snag" through to the GARMENT BACK SIDE.

817. Small holes appear like magic in children's clothes. Cover the hole with a bright patch, applique or iron on the child's name/initial.

Surround it with other and smaller patches, appliques or motifs.

Little kid feels like he's got a brand new shirt.

818. Pin ELASTIC with a BIG SAFETY PIN at the waist on child's clothes.

Child's mother can then make adjustments. It's a good way to make clothes for children who live in another part of the country.

819. Little folks really like the play shirt that has several different color and size buttons sewn on front. Try it on a T-shirt.

Small zippers sewn on the shirt also fascinate the pre-schooler.

820. After my children lost numerous hats at school, I sewed one end of a 1/4" wide length of elastic inside. Other end was pinned to facing of child's coat. No more lost hats.

Make the elastic pretty. Crochet over elastic with contrasting or same color yarn.

821 <u>MONEY SAVER WITH CHILDREN'S PAJAMAS</u> ...

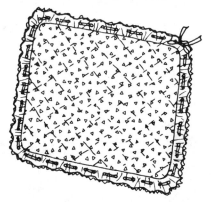

Cut sleeves and legs LONGER than needed. Put elastic in lower edges. Sleeves and legs will blouse a little.

As the child grows, elastic can be removed.

822. Put a small piece of bias or twill tape, care label or child's name label in back of little folks' garments so he/she can distinguish it from the front.

823. ENTERTAIN LITTLE FOLKS when you're sewing ... Make the little one a special box. Cover with contact paper and let the child know it is special for use only when <u>YOU</u> are sewing <u>TOGETHER</u>.

Box can have small play scissors, ruler, fabric scraps, thread spools and miniatures of all the other things "momie" uses.

Such a box kept my children entertained for 30 to 40 minutes.

824. <u>MAKE A MARVELOUS SHOWER GIFT</u> for half the price ...

"Spiff" up a purchased COTTON QUILTED BABY PAD.

Sew a pretty ruffle around the edge. If an eyelet ruffle is used, lace it with ribbon and tie in a bow at one corner.

825. USE SHEET FUSIBLE WEB to

 ...   Apply PATCHES.
 ...   Make SHOULDER PADS.
 ...   Apply APPLIQUES (really a time saver for quilters).
    <u>WARNING</u>:   Keep small scraps away from iron.

826. I have heard children complain about book bag straps cutting into their shoulders.

Rip out a section of the straps and stuff with fiberfill. Padded straps are far more comfortable.

Try padded straps on PURSES, DIAPER and other TOTE BAGS.

On occasion, I have seen a baby being carried on mother's back, with the backpack cutting into a tiny leg. PAD THE LEG HOLE AREA.

827. Fuse INTERFACING to fabric before cutting out appliques. Fraying is minimized and it cuts much easier.

828. APPLY APPLIQUES, using a PLASTIC BAG ...

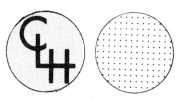

Cut applique shape a little LARGER FROM PLASTIC BAG. (Vegetable bag from the grocery store will do).

Place plastic between applique and fabric. Cover with press cloth. PRESS.

Plastic and heat adheres applique to the fabric.

829. EASIER MACHINE APPLIQUE ... SPRAY STARCH cutout pieces and iron. Piece has more body and doesn't fray easily. Hold in place with GLUE STICK.

830. When doing applique work, place a disposable COFFEE FILTER beneath the fabric before sewing.

Sew fabric and filter. Tear filter off the back.

Adding machine tape also works well on small projects.

831. Cut felt (or other applique) and FUSIBLE WEB at the same time. Use GLUE STICK to hold them together. Web will not slip. Both will be the same "perfect" size.

This will also eliminate little lost web pieces that mess up the iron sole plate and bond your circular skirt to the ironing board WHILE you're wearing it.

832. To test DURABILITY of FELT, pull it in VERTICAL and HORIZONTAL directions. Usually vertical direction is the stronger ... but not always.

Keep in mind thickness of felt does not always mean it is stronger.

833. When making garments from FELT, use simple unlined and collarless patterns.

Facings must be eliminated. They make the garment bulky.

834. OVERLAP seams on FELT ... OR ... BUTT TRIMMED EDGES together. Sew a decorative trim or strip of leather, etc. over butted edges with a topstitch.

835. EDGES on FELT may be BLANKET STITCHED after TRIMMING. Then, crochet garment pieces together, catching blanket stitches.

836. It may be necessary to use TWO THICKNESSES of LIGHT-WEIGHT or LIGHT COLORED fabrics to applique over dark or print fabrics.

837. Keep an EMORY BOARD handy in the sewing area.

It's good for curing NAIL and CUTICLE SNAGS.

It cleans ERASERS.

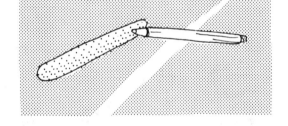

838. Use an EMORY BOARD to file the SMOOTH TIP of your MARK-ING PEN for a little longer wear and use.

839. It will not be necessary to bend over if a MAGNET is glued to the YARDSTICK.

Run it over the carpet to pick up pins.

840. When working on several projects at one time, put each in a plastic dishpan.

Project can be moved from room to room for handwork. Dishpan can be placed on shelf, bookcase, under sewing table, etc.

This avoids clutter; dishpan is a cheerful addition to the sewing room and project items are kept together.

841. Use PATTERNED SHEETS to make DRAPERIES. Very good for children's room and they're already hemmed.

842. SHOWER CURTAINS can be made from POLYESTER KNITS. They shed water, too.

843. PERFECT CORNERS for PILLOWS ...   Stuff corners first.

Put a large SAFETY PIN through each corner to hold stuff- in place.   Stuff remaining body of the pillow.

Corner stuffing will not shift for life of the pillow.

844. ELIMINATE ITCHES ... Sometimes, little particles stick to the skin when working with velvets, sweater, fleece, velour or similar type fabrics.

Rub hands and arms with BOUNCE before starting the project. No more "itches."

845. FOAM STRIPS used to fight static electricity and soften clothes in a dryer may be added to fiberfill for STUFFING PILLOWS, TOYS, etc.

They're soft and smell good long after use in the dryer is depleted.

846. Take guesswork out of the amount of RIBBON or CORDING needed for a project ...

Tie a bow in the same size you expect to use, with **string or yarn.**

Measure the string and **add 1/2"** for a center loop. Multiply times the number of bows needed.

847.   Put a DRAWSTRING around LOWER EDGE of a PICNIC TABLECLOTH. When the wind comes up, pull DRAW- STRINGS and tie securely around UNDER part of the table.

848. ZIGZAG STITCH all edges of WASH- CLOTHS and TOWELS before using.   They will last longer.

849. MAKE NAME TAGS for GIFT PACKAGES ... Trace outline of various notions on construction paper. Cut out and place on package tie.

850. LAUNDRY SOAP BOXES can be cut down and used to store sewing magazines and periodicals.

851. On occasion, KITCHEN PLATES come in handy for tracing CURVES.

852. For a FLATTER STOMACH, EXERCISE when SEWING.

Hold each foot off the floor for several seconds, four or five times.

853. Your "junk" may be another's "treasure." If you're tired of "THAT" piece of fabric, ask sewing friends if they'd like to trade.

Hold a FABRIC SWAP MEET with PATTERN PARTIES. Some-one else may "adore" your "dislike."

854. Use PLASTIC CANVAS instead of cardboard in fabric projects that need support.

It's washable, as well as sturdy and durable.

855. YOU can FIREPROOF CANVAS ... Canvas is a natural fibre and will burn easily.

Mix 1/2 cup AMMONIA PHOSPHATE (buy from a garden supply store in your area), 1 cup AMMONIUM CHLORIDE (at drug stores) and 1 quart WATER.

Mix and put in a "spray" container. Spray canvas hand-bags, chairs, etc.

Re-spray if item gets wet and after each washing.

856. If GLUE used in your craft or sewing projects, has thicken-ed or dried, sometimes adding a little WHITE VINEGAR will soften or thin it out.

857. To control static electricity problems when stuffing pillows, toys, etc., dip fingers in a bowl of water to which one tablespoon WHITE VINEGAR has been added.

Rub hands together to distribute moisture. Repeat as necessary.

858. When planning to sew with VELVET or CORDUROY, choose a simple pattern. Avoid topstitching, pressed pleats and sewn tucks.

859. When lining VELVET, handbaste layers together with a

129

L-O-N-G loose DIAGONAL stitch.   Cut basting threads every 1 1/2" to 2".   Remove.

860. When sewing on VELVET, use a ROLLER or WALKING FOOT. Fabric "shifting" problems will be minimal.

861. Sew VELVET with a SIZE 9 or 10 NEEDLE and use 10 to 12 stitches to the inch.

862. Avoid puckers in seams of FINE fabrics and SHEERS ...

Always sew with a very small needle ... and ... NO BACKSTITCHING.

863. WAXED PAPER placed on top of "plastic" fabrics i.e. VINYL or similar types, will eliminate puckering and needle won't stick.

864. To cut out "CRAWL-LY" fabric (silk, chiffon, sheers, etc.) pin to large sheets of tissue paper.

Pin the pattern and cut through fabric and tissue at the same time.   Leave tissue paper attached to fabric piece and tear away after sewing garment.

Do know it takes longer to work with "crawl-ly" fabrics.

865. Do NOT let NEW THREAD remain in contact with damp fabric for a prolonged period of time.   Excess thread dyes may fade onto the fabric.

866. Place JIFFY GRIP on the bottom of handmade BATHROOM and THROW RUGS.   Keeps them from slipping.

867. If Jiffy Grip is not available for Bathroom and Throw Rugs, sew RUBBER JAR RINGS on the UNDERSIDE.

868. Use COLORED SHOE LACES as DRAWSTRINGS for jacket hoods, etc.   If desired color is not available, buy WHITE ones and DYE.

Sew laces together for longer DRAWSTRINGS.

869. If you're worried whether ZIPPER CENTER back laps LEFT or RIGHT, know it DOES NOT MATTER.

870. Keep a supply of ZIP LOC bags in the sewing room.   They can be used to store notions, single fabric pieces, garments and patterns.

It's easy to see through them and they come in various sizes.

871. Put an EXTRA SET of SEWING TOOLS (pins, needles, nippers etc.) in a Zip Loc Bag to take with you in the car, to doctor's office ... to complete small projects when waiting.

872. Hang a canvas or shopping bag on the ironing board (large end) to hold pressing aids.

873. Just keep in mind COTTON IRONING BOARD covers absorb heat instead of reflecting it.

   Cotton cover should definitely be used when pressing knits.

874. LEAD will not break so easily and MARKING PENCIL will last longer if placed in the FREEZER half hour before sharpening.

875. KEEP CROCHET or KNITTING project clean. Place thread in a regular kitchen ZIP LOC bag. Leave a small opening at the top for thread feed-thru.

876. MAKE EARRINGS from SHANK BUTTONS ... Remove button shank with clippers. File and sand rough areas.

   Glue earring clips to the back. (Tie tacks and pretty pins may be made in this manner also).

877. PRACTICAL CHRISTMAS GIFT for a sewing friend ... Cover a Cigar Box with colorful contact paper. Fill it with sewing notions ... nippers, tapemeasure, pins, needles, etc. A sewing friend will remember you for a long, long time.

878. If your climate is ICE and SNOW and there's no dryer, put a little SALT in the final rinse water.

   Clothes will not stick and freeze on the clothesline.

879. TAKE SEWING CLASSES ... everywhere ... anywhere ... until you feel secure in your ability.

   Start with simple patterns ... ask sewing friends for help ... they will be flattered.

   Watch newspapers and magazines for tidbits of sewing information, not ordinarily taught in classes.

880. Invest a dollar or two for your own printed address labels. Peel off and place on orders, requests for information or free drawings at Sewing, Craft and Quilting affairs. There will be no mistake about your correct name and address.

MAKE IT DO, USE IT UP, WEAR IT OUT

881. Do NOT THROW away SCRAPS until garment is finished. Throw-aways may include one of the garment pieces. (The reason I know?? I lost a sleeve once).

882. Put a SCRAP from each garment in the pattern envelope. It will help you remember which garment was made and if future alterations will be necessary.

883. *** A great use for KNIT SCRAPS ... MAKE YOUR OWN YARN. ... Cut knit scraps into strips, lengthwise. Experiment to find width of strips needed for your project.

Piece the strips together or treat each piece separately for knitting or crochet pattern.

To make the yarn, pull strip taut.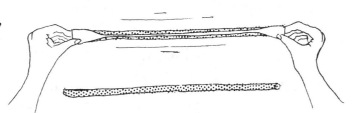

Ends will roll in, creating a smooth tube of fabric.

THAT'S ALL. It can be used to crochet or knit anything from small items to rugs, depending on size of the strips and fineness of the knit.

It's also great for latchet hook projects. It can be cut into pieces for making rugs or soft toys.

884. Cut fabric strips from SCRAPS with PINKING SHEARS. Use to tie CHRISTMAS and other GIFT PACKAGES.

It's less expensive than ribbon and no one will doubt your creativity.

885. An ORDERLY SCRAP BAG ... Do this project on a quiet, rainy day. (On occasion, I feel my scrap bag takes VITA-MINS since it grows so fast).

Divide scraps into piles of cotton, knits, wools, furs, corduroy, etc. Sort by color. Place by type and color

*** Reprinted with permission of
THE NEEDLE PEOPLE NEWS

P. O. Box 115
Syosset, New York 11791

in a ZIP LOC bag.   Label and store.   Craft projects are easier when you can go right to a particular scrap bag.

886. If you do not want SCRAPS, give them to friends or charitable groups for quilting and other patchwork.

887. When there are no SCRAPS for making PIPING, try the husband's tie. (Forgiveness is easier to get than permission).

888. Save small SCRAP BITS of FUSIBLE WEB.   Put them in an envelope or small zip loc bag.

Use to handle "misbehaving" facings, ripped hems and other minor repairs.

889. Make BIAS TAPE from LEFTOVER SCRAPS ... Cut in any width.   Roll onto cardboard.   Just press, when ready to use.

890. MAKING THE MOST of SOAP SCRAPS ...

...   Put soap scraps in toe of a cut off hose foot. (TOE SHOULD BE SHEER). Tie cut end. Wet and use as usual until soap is gone.

...   If Needle Lube isn't available, soap can help the "skipped stitching" problem. Rub on needle, scissors edge, etc.

It is particularly helpful when sewing with heavy fabrics like canvas, denim, corduroy ... rub on area to be sewn.

...   Run sharp edge of soap along seam-line. Stitch on the seamline. Needle goes in and out without "cheating."

...   ZIPPERS work better after "soap-ing." Saw teeth of an old metal zipper, back and forth across soap scrap.

...   Use soap scrap instead of Bees Wax to coat handsewing thread. Run thread back and forth over soap. Helps eliminate knots and tangles.

891. Keep <u>SOAP</u> (that does not have cream base) <u>SCRAPS</u> to make construction marks on dark fabric.

892. Sharpen SOAP edges with scissors blade or emory board.

893.  The "<u>NEW</u>" look <u>will</u> return if <u>LINEN</u> is <u>boiled</u> with <u>PURE SOAP</u> ... use the SCRAPS.

894. SCRAPS from "PILE" fabrics make marvelous SHOESHINE STRIPS or MITS.

(Instructions are in my book <u>66 QUICK GIFTS TO SEW</u>).

They're pretty, make great Christmas Stocking Stuffers and are very effective with shoes.

895. Gift CARDS from the seamstress CAN be a conversation piece.

Cut designs from SCRAPS of last year's favorite fabric. Glue to a folded file card and write your own message.

896. Make <u>COLLARS</u>, <u>CUFFS</u>, <u>TRIMS</u>, etc. from <u>UNUSED HANDKER-CHIEF</u> or <u>SCARF</u>.

897. Convert "your guy's" discarded shirt into a roomy, around-the-house smock for you.

Cut off and hem sleeves just above the placket. If the shirt has a stand and collar, rip off the collar. Leave the "stand" and sew it closed.

If "tabbed" sleeves are preferred, follow directions in Tip No. 794, Page 121.

898. <u>SHORTEN LINGERIE</u> ... Mark desired length. Sew on lace. Cut away excess fabric just under lace stitching. There are no frayed or curled edges to fight.

899. Recycle a half slip that's too SHORT. Turn it <u>UPSIDE, DOWN</u>.

Take in the sides to fit. Add lace or spaghetti straps

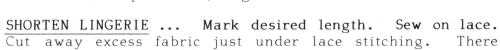

at the shoulders. Makes a nice camisole to wear under sheers. It can hang straight or elastic may be added at the waist.

900. If SLIP (half or whole) is too long, don't CUT it off.

Shorten with small HORIZONTAL tucks. Slip may be lengthened if necessary in the future ... Tucks are also decorative.

If slip is too short, put EXTRA WIDE LACE on the lower edge.

901. Do NOT discard the old IRONING BOARD COVER. Cut PATCHES from usable parts to make heat-resistant backs on handmade POTHOLDERS.

902. If FUSIBLE WEB has gotten OLD and doesn't want to adhere, put strips in WARM WATER and use immediately.

903. WORN MACHINE NEEDLES are still useful ...

Use to hang small, lightweight pictures (instead of nails); they don't leave holes.

Also, pin pattern pieces and/or instruction sheets to the sewing board.

904. When bed pillows get old, fold and sew ends together. Makes a square pillow. Cover with pretty fabric. Beats department store decorative pillow prices.

905. Loved last year's print dress but it has a hole five inches down from the left shoulder?

Make a PILLOW out of the skirt. No money spent and you still have an "eyepleaser."

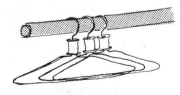

906. Do NOT throw away SMALL THREAD SPOOLS ...

Use on CLOTHES HANGERS to keep clothing separated in the closet.

907. Spray THREAD SPOOLS with gold, silver or other Christmas-color paint.

Run ribbon or yarn through the spool and tie to the Christmas Tree limbs. Saves money not spent on breakable bulbs.

Your holiday friends will have no doubt that
you are a true FABRIC ARTIST.

908. THREAD EMPTY SPOOLS on to a TRIPLE STRAND
of DENTAL FLOSS.

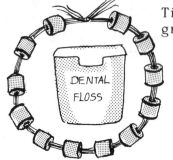

Tie floss ends together.   They   make
great TOYS for little folks.

** WOODEN SPOOLS are now ANTIQUES.
Don't thow them away.

909. EMPTY   THREAD   SPOOLS   may
substitute   for   DRAWER   PULLS
on children's furniture.

910. Reuse THREAD removed from an original HEM. It was
already made to match the garment.

Iron it first, to get rid of wrinkles, krinkles and curls
or you'll get tangles and frustration.

911. Use ULTRA SUEDE (RTM) (instead of leather) for ELBOW
PATCHES on jackets, sweaters, yokes, etc.

It makes marvelous decorative yokes and cuffs on Western
style shirts. Easy to sew and WASHABLE.

912. Make PLACEMATS from discarded, unusable DRAPERIES.

913. Recycle old UMBRELLA CLOTH COVERING. It's waterproof
and makes an excellent lining for purses and tote bags.

914. Make WASHCLOTHS from frayed towels.

915. Cut off TOE SEAMS of PANTYHOSE/NYLONS. Use only the
sheer leg part.

Pad WOODEN HANGERS by wrapping with
the "leg."

Use as many as necessary to get desired padding. Cover
hanger with a pretty print.

Complete instructions for making COVERED HANGERS are
in my book   66 QUICK GIFTS TO SEW.

916. Cut off PANYHOSE/NYLON seams. Cut sheer parts into small
squares. STUFF PILLOWS, TOYS, TUBE SOCKS (for sleeve
rolls), etc. Item can be washed and dries quickly.

917. Use CANNED AIR to "blow" lint out of the sewing machine. Don't let the children play with it; it scares the dogs and cats "spitless."

918. To reflect more LIGHT, put a MIRROR on the wall beside the sewing machine.

919. Doctors' Examination Table PAPER is great for tracing PATTERNS. Visit the local surgical supply house.

920. If additional SEAM ALLOWANCE is necessary for pattern adjustment, use the TAPEMEASURE as a guide.

   Tapemeasure is exactly 5/8" wide ... same as the standard seam allowance.

   Lay tapemeasure on the seamline and trace new cutting line. Works nicely around curves, too.

921. Use a PAPER CLIP CADDY for PINS. Magnetic ring at the top keeps pins lined up around the rim for handy use.

922. FLAMING BRIGHT color IRONING BOARD COVER makes it a little easier to see garment details i.e. seams, notches, etc.

923. Use current IRONING BOARD COVER as a pattern to make one from TERRY CLOTH just for pressing NAPPED FABRIC.

924. CENTER CREASE in COTTON KNITS "may be helped" and sometimes removed by spraying with MAGIC SIZING (R), manufactured by ARMOUR-DIAL. Check the grocery store.

925. Treat SEERSUCKER fabrics the same as a stripe. Ripples have same effect as a stripe.

926. EYEGLASSES CASE can be made quickly by folding a QUILTED POTHOLDER in half. Sew together at one end and the side.

927. Make an inexpensive EVENING CLUTCH. Sew sequins and beads to a COSMETIC BAG.

928. Cut out GOOD parts of old CROCHETED DOILIES and make a potpourri sachet. Trim with lace, braid, etc.

929. No one wears shoes that are too tight.   If you have
     the problem with <u>REAL LEATHER</u> shoes, SOAK them in
     warm water about 25 minutes.

     Blot excess water with a clean towel. Wear shoes until
     dry. They won't hurt anymore.

930. Instead of putting buttons on the blouse CUFF, make
     a buttonhole on each side.   Pass ribbon, tubing or
     tiny strap through both buttonholes and tie ... <u>OR</u>
     ... sew tubing, ribbon or straps in the cuff side seams
     and tie. Very pretty.

931. When Bra Cup is Size "B" or larger, garment darts
     should be <u>SLANTED</u> (not horizontal).

     Horizontal darts are fine for smaller busts.

932. Small square SCRAPS of ULTRA SUEDE (R) Brand Fabric
     may be used as blouse <u>STAYS</u> inside skirt and trouser
     waistband.

     Attach stays to each side before sewing band to the
     garment.

     Stay does not add bulk and is WASHABLE.

933. There's about one yard for every two rolls of fabric
     (medium weight) on the bolt.

     Before unrolling, count the number of rolls to see if
     there's enough for your project.   Divide number of
     "rolls" by two i.e. 6 rolls = 3 yards (about).

     Doesn't work with sheers or bulkies.

934. Use <u>EMPTY BAND AID CANS</u> to store small things and
     "little LOSABLES."

935. Carry small FOLDING SCISSORS in your handbag for
     "snipping" fabric swatches, clipping threads, etc.
     They do come in handy.

936. <u>BUTTONHOLES</u> for ladies are sewn on <u>RIGHT HAND SIDE</u>
     <u>of the garment.</u>   Just remember <u>"ladies are ALWAYS</u>
     <u>RIGHT</u>."

     Buttonholes for men are always on the <u>LEFT</u>.

     I've "blown it" a time or two. If it happens to you,
     just sew buttonhole together.   Sew button on top of
     your "goof."

937. Before children wear new purchased garments, re-enforce BUTTONS by sewing with dental floss. Saves frustration when buttons drop off as child goes out the door. Saves lost buttons, too.

938. MONOGRAMS should be placed in CENTER of the POCKET. If there's no pocket, it should be 3" – 4" up from waist on the LEFT.

939. Small pins fall out of MESH, LOOSE WEAVE and NET fabrics. Use HAT or FLORIST PINS.

940. CLOTHES CARE ...

   ... Clothes last longer if cleaned regularly, especially if exposed to cosmetics and perfume.
   ... Do NOT store clothes in DAMP or HOT areas.
   ... Use SHAPED HANGERS for JACKETS and COATS.
   ... Clothes are brighter, cleaner and softer if washed in soft or conditioned water.
   ... When washing clothes, do not OVERload nor UNDERload the washer. UNDERloading results in inadequate agitation and clothes do not come clean.

941. NEVER fit garments WRONG side, out. Wrong side will be adjusted.

942. Put the SEWING MACHINE on a portable TV table. It can be rolled from room to room.

943. Go to the toy store and buy a "little girl's BROOM." It's handy for cleaning the sewing room ... takes up less space, too.

944. CORRECT WIDTH FOR HEMS ... Coats about 2". Dresses and skirts, about 1 1/2". Circular skirt is an exception. (See Tip No. 740).

945. Always apply INTERFACING to FRONT FACINGS before sewing darts in the garment pieces. It's much quicker.

946. After cutting out a high pile fabric like fake fur, put the pieces in a dryer for 60 seconds. Pieces will be rid of excess "pile." Pieces are easier to sew.

947. Use colored HAIR SETTING TAPE for PATTERN ALTERATIONS. It doesn't get brittle, crack or peel off the pattern.

948. JACKET or COAT SLEEVE may be shortened by taking a tuck in the LINING. Tuck may be removed later if necessary to lengthen the sleeve.

949. Keep a PENCIL SHARPENER among your "sewing gear." Pencils DO wear out. Also, you can use pencil lead to rub on zippers for smoother "zipping."

950. Bend a TINY, FINE COPPER WIRE into a loop. Makes a great NEEDLE THREADER.

BE CONSIDERATE OF FABRIC SHOP PERSONNEL
They may be the very best friends
you have when sewing help is needed.

ALWAYS REMEMBER ... AS YE SEW, SO SHALL YE R-I-P

FABRIC CONVERSION CHART (Yardage and Metric)

- Figures are approximate.
- Extra fabric will be needed for one way designs or nap fabrics.
- Large fabric designs, pattern alterations, unusual shape or large pattern pieces may require changes in yardage requirements.

FABRIC WIDTH	35"-36" (90 cm)	39" (100 cm)	41" (104 cm)	44"-45" (115 cm)	50" (127 cm)	52"-54" (140 cm)	58"-60" (150 cm)	66" (168 cm)
	1¾ (1.60 m)	1½ (1.40 m)	1½ (1.40 m)	1⅜ (1.30 m)	1¼ (1.10 m)	1⅛ (1.00 m)	1 (0.90 m)	⅞ (.80 m)
	2 (1.80 m)	1¾ (1.60 m)	1¾ (1.60 m)	1⅝ (1.50 m)	1½ (1.40 m)	1⅜ (1.30 m)	1¼ (1.10 m)	1⅛ (1.00 m)
	2¼ (2.10 m)	2 (1.80 m)	2 (1.80 m)	1¾ (1.60 m)	1⅝ (1.50 m)	1½ (1.40 m)	1⅜ (1.30 m)	1¼ (1.10 m)
	2½ (2.30 m)	2¼ (2.10 m)	2¼ (2.10 m)	2⅛ (1.90 m)	1¾ (1.60 m)	1¾ (1.60 m)	1⅝ (1.50 m)	1½ (1.40 m)
	2⅞ (2.60 m)	2½ (2.30 m)	2½ (2.30 m)	2¼ (2.10 m)	2 (1.80 m)	1⅞ (1.70 m)	1¾ (1.60 m)	1⅝ (1.50 m)
	3⅛ (2.90 m)	2¾ (2.50 m)	2¾ (2.50 m)	2½ (2.30 m)	2¼ (2.10 m)	2 (1.80 m)	1⅞ (1.70 m)	1¾ (1.60 m)
	3⅜ (3.10 m)	3 (2.70 m)	2⅞ (2.60 m)	2¾ (2.50 m)	2⅜ (2.20 m)	2¼ (2.10 m)	2 (1.80 m)	1⅞ (1.70 m)
	3¾ (3.40 m)	3¼ (3.00 m)	3⅛ (2.90 m)	2⅞ (2.60 m)	2⅝ (2.40 m)	2⅜ (2.20 m)	2¼ (2.10 m)	2⅛ (1.90 m)
	4¼ (3.90 m)	3½ (3.20 m)	3⅜ (3.10 m)	3⅛ (2.90 m)	2¾ (2.50 m)	2⅝ (2.40 m)	2⅜ (2.20 m)	2¼ (2.10 m)
	4½ (4.10 m)	3¾ (3.40 m)	3⅝ (3.30 m)	3⅜ (3.10 m)	3 (2.70 m)	2¾ (2.50 m)	2⅝ (2.40 m)	2½ (2.30 m)
	4¾ (4.30 m)	4 (3.70 m)	3⅞ (3.50 m)	3⅝ (3.30 m)	3¼ (3.00 m)	2⅞ (2.60 m)	2¾ (2.50 m)	2⅝ (2.40 m)
	5 (4.60 m)	4¼ (3.90 m)	4⅛ (3.80 m)	3⅞ (3.50 m)	3⅜ (3.10 m)	3⅛ (2.90 m)	2⅞ (2.60 m)	2¾ (2.50 m)

YOUR PERSONAL MEASUREMENTS

DATE _____

BUST (Over fullest point and DO wear a good Bra)   _____

HIGH BUST (Around Body, UNDER the ARMS. Be
     sure tapemeasure is straight across   _____
     the back).

SHOULDER (from NECK base bone to SHOULDER
     bone. See Tip 276, Page 41).   _____

BACK WIDTH (From Arm crease to Arm crease).   _____

NECK (Around the Neck Base).   _____

UPPER ARM (Around fullest part).   _____

ARM LENGTH (From Shoulder Bone edge to Wrist
     with arm in slightly bent position).   _____

WAIST (Use a Cord if necessary. See Tip 273,
     Page 40).   _____

BACK WAIST LENGTH (from Neck Base Bone to
     Waist).   _____

FRONT WAIST LENGTH (from Shoulder center over
     the Bust to Waist).   _____

HIPS (Around largest part, usually 9" below
     the Waistline).   _____

CROTCH LENGTH (From Center Front Waist through
     the crotch to center Back Waist).   _____

CROTCH DEPTH (Sit on table with knees together.   _____
     Place hands on knees. Measure
     straight down from waist to table
     top. DO NOT tuck tapemeasure
     under the hip.

NOTES

- - - - - - - - - - - - - - - - - - Cut here and mail - - - - - - - - - - - - - - - - - -

All shipments made promptly

O R D E R

To: SEW KNO-HOW
      P. O. Box 12102
      Fresno, CA 93776

Please send:

_____ copies SUPER QUICK SEWING TIPS (Rev. Ed.) @ $8.95 ea. $ _____

_____ copies 19 SHIRTS FROM ONE PATTERN .... @ $10.95 ea. $ _____

_____ copies 66 QUICK GIFTS TO SEW .... @ $10.95 ea. $ _____

_____   6-WAY BLOUSE PATTERN .... @ $5.95 ea. $ _____

               California Residents add 6 % sales Tax _____

Postage & Handling.   Add $1.00 for each item UNDER $10.00.
                      Add $1.50 for each item OVER $10.00.

               TOTAL ENCLOSED .... $ _____

SHIP TO: Name _____

           Address _____

           _____ _____ _____
           City   State   Zip

/___/ Charge to Visa A/C No. _____   Expires _____

       SIGNATURE _____

143

INDEX

INDEX

INDEX

147

INDEX

148

INDEX

	TIP NO.	PAGE NO.

INDEX

INDEX

INDEX

INDEX

INDEX

INDEX

INDEX

INDEX

INDEX

INDEX

159

INDEX

INDEX

INDEX

163

INDEX

INDEX

INDEX

INDEX

INDEX

INDEX

169

INDEX

INDEX

	TIP NO.	PAGE NO.

INDEX

INDEX

173

175

INDEX

INDEX

	TIP NO.	PAGE NO.

SHEERS (cont'd)

	TIP NO.	PAGE NO.
as Button Cover	684	104
Buttonholes in	698	106
Collars	540	81
Cuffs	540	81
Cutting	864	130
Darts on	419	62
Facings on	395, 540	57, 81
Fusible Web on	170	26
Hemming	732, 738, 751, 752, 753	113, 114, 116
Interfacing for	298, 306	44, 45
Pressing	306	45
Puckers in	862	130
Ruffles	494, 497	74, 75
Shoulder Pads from	501	75
Stitching	396	58
Straps from, turning	450	67
Trimming Seam Allowance	540, 548	81, 82
Underwear under	786	120

SHEETS

for Cleanup	234	34
for Draperies	841	127
for Storage	792	121

SHINE, fixing — 260 — 37

SHIRRING

with Elastic Thread	431	64
Spacing	717	110

SHOE LACES, as Drawstrings — 868 — 130

SHOES, LEATHER (too tight) — 929 — 138

SHOPPING TIME — 761 — 117

SHOULDER FIT — 276 — 41

SHOULDER PADS,

Adding	504	76
Covering	501	75
Eliminating	504	76
Fusible Web for	825	125
Interchangeable	503	76
Location	502	75
Washing	504	76

SHOULDERS

Matching Plaids at	458	69
Width Camouflage	770	119
Yokes	812	123

SHOWER CURTAINS from Knits — 842 — 128

SILK

Chloride salt, effect on	35	8
Drying, air	36	8

177

INDEX

178

INDEX

INDEX

INDEX

181

INDEX

INDEX

INDEX

INDEX

INDEX

INDEX

INDEX